101 Most Puzzling Bible Verses

TIM DEMY & GARY STEWART

HARVEST HOUSE PUBLISHERS

EUGENE, OREGON

All views expressed are solely those of the authors and do not reflect the position or endorsement of any governmental agency or department, military or otherwise.

Cover by Terry Dugan Design, Minneapolis, Minnesota

101 MOST PUZZLING BIBLE VERSES
Copyright © 2006 by Timothy J. Demy and Gary P. Stewart
Published by Harvest House Publishers
Eugene, Oregon 97402

Demy, Timothy J.
   101 most puzzling Bible verses / Tim Demy and Gary Stewart
        p. cm.
   Includes bibliographical references.
   ISBN-13: 978-0-7369-1775-9 (pbk.)
   ISBN-10: 0-7369-1775-6
   1. Bible—Criticism, interpretation, etc. 2. Apologetics. I. Stewart, Gary (Gary P.) II. Title
   BS511.3.D46 2006
   220.6—dc22

Printed in the United States of America

06 07 08 09 10 11 12 13 14 / BP-CF / 10 9 8 7 6 5 4 3 2 1

From Tim: To the memory of "W" (Wayland) Broyles (1953–1990),
faithful in friendship and the service of the Lord.
Your wisdom and laughter are missed daily.

From Gary: To the memory of Kristen Eileen Lewinski (1970–2005).
"Cricket,"
we will miss your smile and voice,
and we will never forget your courage and faith.

Contents

Introduction

Reading the Bible should be fun, not frustrating! "What does that mean?" "I wonder why it says that." "Why is that there?" If you have ever asked one of these or similar questions while reading the Bible, this book is for you. The Bible clearly teaches that each and every verse and passage in it is not only inspired by God but also personally beneficial for you (2 Timothy 3:16-17).

Whether you are casually reading through passages, glancing at verses, or engaged in a detailed Bible study, every interaction with the Bible can yield personal and spiritual benefits. Every reading is an important reading! Yet not every reading yields the clarity or instant comprehension we desire.

Sometimes as we cruise through a verse, a passage, or a chapter, we hit a scriptural speed bump that forces us to slow down, stop, or take a closer look. These speed bumps are verses that for a variety of reasons (cultural, historical, or doctrinal) may not immediately offer a clear meaning or interpretation. In any journey through the Bible, such speed bumps are present, but they, like any small obstacle in the road, are easily overcome with skill and assistance.

God did not give us the Bible to confuse us, but rather to help and encourage us in our daily lives and walk with Him. The verses we have selected are some of the puzzling verses that readers commonly encounter.

Our desire is to provide clear and straightforward explanations of these sometimes troubling verses so you can smoothly continue your journey with God. These pages provide concise presentations and synopses of the verses rather than detailed studies. We are trying to provide short solutions to puzzling verses and not exhaustive (or exhausting) answers! Many resources are available for the latter, and we have listed some of the most helpful at the end of the book in the "Digging Deeper" pages. Pick a verse and see what you think. God wants you satisfied, not confused!

GENESIS 1:27

And God created man in His own image,
in the image of God He created him;
male and female He created them.

> **How do we look like God? What does it**
> **mean to be created in God's image?**

The distinct and unbridgeable chasm between God the Creator and His creation is one of the central teachings of the Bible. Whenever that distinction gets blurred, the intellectual consequences are disastrous. We are not one with the world, or one with God, or becoming God or gods. But Genesis 1:27 reminds us that God and humanity do share some similarities.

Of all the creatures God made, the Bible says He made only one, humans, in His image. In the ancient Near Eastern world, false gods and idols were easily distinguished because their physical characteristics reflected their alleged activities and domains. In contrast to these pagan idols of carved stone and wood, Genesis 1:26-27 states that the true God miraculously created humans in His image. Idols were often made in the likeness of humans, but God turns that upside down (as He does with all secular thought) and creates people in His image.

Being created in God's image means that people are like Him in certain ways (but never identical to Him) and they represent Him in the world. The image of God in humanity is multidimensional with spiritual, moral, mental, and relational aspects.

Every person shares equally in possessing the image of God. God is a spirit, so the image is not a physical representation. Rather, it is found in the human capacity for moral and ethical decision making, conscience, emotions, and spirituality. Just as children's character, values, personality, emotions, and perspectives are much like their parents', so humans (though imperfectly) share many of the traits God possesses. Traits such as life, personality, love, justice, and holiness are attributes that God shared, though imperfectly, with humans.

In part, it is because humans are created in the image of God that the Bible places such a high value on human life, and the reckless destruction of human life is so serious a sin. Although the image of God in humans has been distorted by humanity's fall in the Garden of Eden, it has not been lost, and it remains in each of us. Every person has inherent dignity and infinite worth, and these cross all racial, gender, ethnic, and economic boundaries. No person, born or unborn, young or old, rich or poor, has more value than another.

Our culture is very image conscious. We are fascinated with the superficial glitz and glamour of Hollywood, designer fashions, and pop icons. Celebrities and stars have great influence. From the concert stage to the sports field, we look for people to admire and emulate. The quest for the best means the right job, the right crowd, the right clubs, and the right looks. Yet all of that means nothing to God. Regardless of your possessions, appearance, capabilities, or limitations, God says you already have the best. You are created in His image—you are inexpressibly valuable to Him.

TJD

DON'T MESS WITH DEMONS

~ ✱ ~

GENESIS 6:2

The sons of God saw that the daughters of men were beautiful; and they took wives for themselves, whomever they chose.

Who were the "sons of God"?

Genesis 6:2-4 is a remarkable snapshot of ancient human history, and scholars debate its interpretation. It appears in the context of God's grief over the widespread human wickedness that led to the flood of Noah (Genesis 6:1-13). The depth and breadth of human rebellion against God was so great that God destroyed the human race, except for the remnant of Noah's family in the ark. This section contrasts the fate of the pre-flood world and the fate of Noah; the former received judgment, and the latter, grace. The pre-flood corruption includes the marrying and union of the "sons of God" with the "daughters of men."

In the Bible, the Hebrew phrase translated "sons of God" can mean either people (Deuteronomy 14:1; 32:5; Psalm 73:15; Hosea 1:10) or angels (Job 1:6; 2:1; 38:7; Psalm 29:1; 89:6). The phrase occurs twice in Genesis 6:2-4, and its interpretation helps determine the identity of the Nephilim in 6:4 (a word used again only in Numbers 13:33, where it clearly refers to humans). The "sons of God" are likely either despotic rulers controlled or indwelt by fallen angels, or fallen angels in human bodies. If the "sons of God" are understood as angels here (as has been the prevailing view through the centuries), then they are among the group of fallen angels that followed Satan in his rebellion against God (Isaiah 14:12-20; Ezekiel 28:16-19; Jude 6).

Like Satan, these angels overstepped their bounds by seizing that which was not theirs—in this case, human wives. Likewise, some humans (though we don't know how many), in an act reminiscent of Adam and Eve partaking of the forbidden fruit (Genesis 3:1-7), also overstepped their bounds and cohabitated with the angels. The angels in human bodies tried to seize part of creation, and the humans tried to seize divinity. One of the results of the union was the birth of the Nephilim, ancient heroes who appeared on earth after the marriage (6:4). This and other activities were so abhorrent that God responded to this widespread evil by limiting His protection of humanity and ultimately judging all of creation except for Noah and his family (6:5-8). (Jesus taught in Matthew 22:30 that angels do not marry, but His point was that there is no marriage in heaven. Marriage is limited to earth. He was not talking about this perversion of marriage on earth.)

The passage does not tell us how widespread the practice was, but the implication from the population growth mentioned in Genesis 6:1 is that the sons of God took all they wished. Evil and the human family were both multiplying.

The Nephilim may well be part of the source of the legends and mythology that survive to the present day. The world after the flood was very different from the one before the flood. Throughout the centuries and generations after the flood, the memory of that world became distorted and the Nephilim, mighty men and mythic figures, came to be seen as gods. But they were not gods. The passage is also a polemic against ancient pagan belief that kings and mighty warriors had divine origins. Without the truths of the Bible, everything in life, including history, becomes distorted.

TJD

3

AN UNCHANGING GOD
~ ✵ ~

GENESIS 6:6

*The LORD was sorry that He made man on
the earth, and He was grieved in His heart.*

**Does God change His mind? If He does,
how can we be sure of His promises?**

Several times in the Bible (including 1 Samuel 15:29; Psalm 110:4; Malachi 3:6; and James 1:17), Scripture declares that one of God's primary character traits is His unchanging nature. This truth is very reassuring in the midst of personal struggles and a fast-changing world, for among other things, it assures us that regardless of what happens, God is firm in His love for us, and His promises are true. The theological term for this divine attribute is *immutability*.

Yet other verses (such as Exodus 32:14; 1 Samuel 15:11; Jeremiah 26:3,13; and Jonah 3:10) seem to indicate that God changes His mind at times or can be persuaded to do so by the prayers or actions of humans. How can that be? Is God either indecisive or wrong? If so, then maybe His character is flawed, and He is untrustworthy.

After Adam and Eve left the Garden of Eden, most of their descendents strayed from a relationship with God and filled the world with disobedience, evil, and corruption. As a result of this widespread human rebellion, God commanded Noah to build the ark and fill it with animals and his family, after which God judged the world through the flood. In this context we read for the first time about God being sorry or grieving—in this instance, about the creation of humans.

God is indeed unchanging in His being and essential nature, that is, His promises, purposes, and perfections. He is never inconsistent in His actions, and He is never growing or developing in His person. Yet neither is God robotic or immobile or inactive. God is personal, not impersonal, and therefore He interacts with us, has emotions, and responds accordingly to different situations.

Thus, God sometimes promised something or decreed a certain course or action or outcome. He will not retract those statements or promises, nor will He relent from a declared course of action. Some of God's decrees or intentions are unconditional—they are certain to come to pass (Genesis 22:16-18; 26:3; Psalm 89:3-4). God has an overall plan for the world and for individuals that can never be thwarted.

At other times God states intentions that He is willing to change His mind about in reaction to human response. Examples of this include Exodus 32:12-14, where Moses intervened on behalf of the Israelites who were worshipping the golden calf, and God intended to destroy them. In Jonah 3:9-10; 4:2, God relented from destroying Nineveh after its inhabitants repented. Sometimes God decrees a course of action or outcome, and it will not change. Other times God patiently waits and responds in love and mercy to human actions and prayers.

Genesis 6:6 faithfully records a glimpse of God's emotion in response to circumstances. It provides a snapshot of people as a whole, as they existed at that moment. If they had changed, God would have changed the expression of His attitude or His course of action. God responds differently, though never unjustly or contradictorily, in different situations. This verse is an expression of present displeasure toward human sinfulness.

The verse is also a reminder to all people that we are not alone in the world. We have a God who cares very much about each of us.

TJD

4

DEADLY DECISIONS

~ ✵ ~

GENESIS 9:6

*Whoever sheds man's blood, by man
his blood shall be shed, for in the
image of God He made man.*

Does God prescribe capital
punishment for murderers?

The issue of capital punishment is hotly contested today both within
and outside Christian circles. The slightest knowledge of the history of
capital punishment reveals numerous misjudgments, abuses, and sadly,
pomp when it comes to execution. However, these failings are symptoms
of humanity's shortcomings more than they are the shortcomings of the
punishment. The abuses tend to cause disillusion with the punishment
rather than correction of the human flaws.

The context of this verse is essential to understanding the responsibility God gives to humankind to police itself. Since the time of Adam,
humanity's desire for divine power and prestige had not abated. Rather
than return to God, fallen humanity continued its natural tendency to
seek its own way. Over the years, humanity had turned so far from God
that He declared that the "wickedness of man was great on the earth,
and that every intent of the thoughts of his heart was only evil continually" (Genesis 6:5). The subsequent verses (Genesis 6:6–8:22) depict the
universal destruction of humankind by means of the great flood. Sin had
become so all-encompassing that God regretted having created man at
all (Genesis 6:6). For the sake of future generations, He was forced to

bring a corrupt generation to the grave, less eight souls. Noah and his family were spared, and God established a new covenant with them (Genesis 9:1-17).

In the Noachian covenant or agreement we see God's love of humanity as well as His regard for the animal kingdom. The covenant restates and reestablishes God's relationship with humankind after the flood: God established seasons as natural indications of His promise not to destroy "every living thing" (Genesis 8:21-22); Noah and his family were to become the parents of future generations, thus establishing anew a "brotherhood" of human beings (see Genesis 9:1,5 and note the word "brother"); God once again gave humanity dominion over the animal kingdom (Genesis 9:2-3); a rainbow became a perpetual sign to every living thing that disembarked the ark that God would never again deploy water to destroy the earth (Genesis 9:8-17); and finally, and most pertinent to our discussion, God placed such value on human life that any animal or human being who took it would forfeit its own life (Genesis 9:4-6).

Genesis 9:6 clearly states that as long as men and women are made or created in the image of God, capital punishment administered by human hands ("by man his blood shall be shed") is required. No longer will God be solely responsible for the containment of evil that lies in the heart of every man "from his youth" (Genesis 8:21). Humankind, whether through the vengeance of family members and city elders in Israelite society (Deuteronomy 19:11-13; Joshua 20) or through a sensible and just government in modern times (Romans 13:1-6; 1 Peter 2:13-14), is responsible for ensuring that human life is held in the highest esteem, so much so that the one who dares to commit murder understands that his vile and arrogant act is, in fact, an act of suicide—life for a life.

God's destruction of human life in the flood was not to be misunderstood as a devaluing of human life. This aspect of the Noahic covenant ensures that humankind gives human life its honored place in the realm of created things. Because God loves humanity, He intervened to stop man's "darker side" from spiraling beyond control to ultimate annihilation, and our love for one another demands we protect the sanctity of human life by establishing capital laws that punish those who in passion or premeditation desire to end the life of another.

Tolerance of such a destructive and despicable act as murder naturally leads to a greater tolerance and acceptance of other inappropriate or selfish behaviors. Divorce, adultery, abortion, and homosexuality are now acceptable behaviors and reflect humanity's natural inclination to satisfy all its desires for power, control, and self-interest—the kind of wickedness that grieves the heart of God. Sin is a malignancy in society that when unimpeded spreads until it contaminates the whole. Human nature without moral boundaries becomes more corrupt and redefines freedom as license. Punishment for inappropriate behavior is administered not primarily as a deterrent, but as a reminder to us all that we each possess a built-in darker side, a cancer, which seeks to diminish, devalue, and destroy human life. Punishment is also a method to rid society through imprisonment and, when necessary, by execution, of those whose actions destroy and denigrate human relationships and life. (The Old Testament discusses unintentional killing in Deuteronomy 19:3-7 and Joshua 20:1-9.)

Capital punishment is not limited to Genesis 9:6. Other passages in the Old Testament include Exodus 21:12 ("He who strikes a man so that he dies shall surely be put to death") and Numbers 35:30-34 ("If anyone kills a person, the murderer shall be put to death at the evidence of witnesses, but no person shall be put to death on the testimony of one witness").

The New Testament also accepts the role of the government to protect society from evil and to enforce justice through capital punishment. In fact, the execution of justice by the state allows its private citizens to follow the tenets Jesus clearly set in the Sermon on the Mount to "not resist evil" and to "turn the other cheek" (see also 2 Corinthians 10:4-5: "for the weapons of our warfare are not of the flesh, but divinely powerful for the destruction of fortresses"). It is the state's responsibility to implement the peace by force when necessary, which includes capital punishment (Luke 19:27; 20:9-16; Acts 25:11; Romans 13:1-7). These passages clearly delineate the difference between personal and social ethics, which are intended to work together for the safety and betterment of all society.

No one can deny that injustices with regard to capital punishment exist—innocent victims have been executed. The goal, however, is not to eliminate a just punishment, but to improve on the evidence and methods used to prove guilt. Certainty is essential to a guilty verdict. Each citizen is responsible to participate in trials as jurors when asked, if for no other reason than to ensure that evidence is solid and doubts are fully addressed. Justice must be well served. When certainty is unobtainable, lesser judgments or acquittals are not only appropriate, they are required. And when a guilty verdict is reached and the sentence is death, celebration of any kind is wholly inappropriate. Nothing is gratifying in the loss of life, not even in the death of a vicious, vile, and murderous scoundrel. Death is the enemy of us all.

GPS

5
THE GREATEST TEST
~ ❋ ~

GENESIS 22:2

He said, "Take now your son, your only son,
whom you love, Isaac, and go to the land of
Moriah, and offer him there as a burnt offering
on one of the mountains of which I will tell you."

Why did God tell Abraham to offer his son Isaac as a human sacrifice?

When God called Abraham (originally named Abram) out of the land of Ur (present-day Iraq), He promised Abraham that his lineage would become a great nation (Genesis 12:1-3). Yet in Genesis 22:2, God commands Abraham to kill and sacrifice the son who was born to Abraham and his wife, Sarah.

The pagan religions of the ancient Near East, such as those of the Canaanites and Phoenicians, practiced the ritual of child sacrifice in their worship of fertility gods. These gods were supposedly entitled to a portion of all that had been produced, whether grain, animals, or children. However, God expressly condemned and forbade child sacrifice (Leviticus 18:21), and anyone who practiced it was to be stoned to death (Leviticus 20:2-5). Nevertheless, child sacrifice did occur among the Israelites in acts of disobedience and idolatry (2 Kings 16:3).

Why then did God tell Abraham to perform such a horrific act? After many years of infertility, Abraham and Sarah were blessed with a son, Isaac. Isaac was a gift from God and the beginning of the fulfillment of God's unconditional promise to Abraham that he would be the progenitor of a great people. Now, in the greatest test of Abraham's life, God was asking him to give back his son. God was testing Abraham, asking him to do something that defied all logic. Genesis 22:1 tells readers that this event was a test, but that doesn't mean Abraham knew it was a test.

The Hebrew word used here for *test* occurs eight times in the Old Testament in connection with God's laws or commandments (Exodus 15:22-26; 16:4; 20:18-20; Deuteronomy 8:2,16; Judges 2:21-23; 3:1-4; 2 Chronicles 32:31; Psalm 26:2). When used in reference to a test by God, the word never carries any sense of entrapment or deceit. Rather, it is always an issue of obedience and faithfulness. God was secretly testing Abraham's obedience and faith. He was calling Abraham to put his faith into action, his words into deeds.

God used this test to strengthen Abraham's faith and his relationship with God. Just as Abraham loved Isaac and had a special relationship with him, so also God loved Abraham as His son and had a special relationship with him. And testing is one of the ways God carries out His purposes and plans. God only tests those He loves, and He does so not to hurt them or tempt them, but to strengthen them. God tests us to help us, not to harm us.

Abraham succeeded in this test, and God prevented Isaac's death, providing an animal sacrifice instead (Genesis 22:12-13). By passing the greatest test in his life, Abraham demonstrated the truth of James 1:3 that "the testing of your faith produces endurance."

TJD

6

HARD AS NAILS AND COLD AS ICE

~ ✻ ~

EXODUS 9:12

*And the LORD hardened Pharaoh's heart,
and he did not listen to them, just as
the LORD had spoken to Moses.*

Why did God harden Pharaoh's heart?

If you have ever seen concrete poured for a foundation or sidewalk and observed it slowly hardening, you have a sense of what happened to the ruler of Egypt during the ten plagues that came upon him and his country when God freed the Israelites from slavery. Like the concrete that slowly hardens with each passing minute, so too did Pharaoh's stubbornness and rebellion against God harden with each new plague. Each plague brought a continuation of willful obstinacy.

The amazing story of that deliverance and the miracles of the plagues is recorded in Exodus 7:14–12:36. Just after the sixth plague, the Bible first records God's hardening of Pharaoh's heart. It is particularly perplexing because the Bible also says that the king hardened his own heart, stubbornly refusing God's wishes (Exodus 7:13-14,22; 8:15,19,32; 9:34-35; 13:15). What happened this time?

Before the plagues started, God told Moses that He would harden Pharaoh's heart (Exodus 4:21; 7:3), and eight times during the plagues the Bible states that God fulfilled His declaration (Exodus 9:12; 10:1,20,27; 11:10; 14:4,8,17). At first glance we might wonder if God authors evil and then holds someone else responsible, but such is not the case. With each new plague, Pharaoh hardened his heart more against God. Rather

21

than seeing God's miraculous works and repenting, he saw them and became more determined to reject God. Only then did God say in effect, "let it be so." God did not violate Pharaoh's moral freedom. Nor did God cause Pharaoh to act contrary to his own desires or natural impulses. God finished what Pharaoh started. God's hardening of Pharaoh's heart was an act of judgment that Pharaoh brought on himself for the mistreatment of the Hebrew slaves. It was not something that God did because He was fickle, impatient, or arbitrary.

God sent the plagues on the Egyptians primarily to display His power so that all who saw it might believe in God (Exodus 6:7; 7:5; 9:16; 10:1-2; 11:9; 14:4,17-18), although from the human vantage point it seemed that the purpose was the freedom of the slaves. God's actions and His plans and purposes are greater than human understanding. And the plagues fulfilled God's desire. Pharaoh's own magicians recognized that God was behind the plagues, and when the Israelites left Egypt, many other people accompanied them (Exodus 12:38).

God did not manipulate Pharaoh and then punish him. Pharaoh retained his own accountability and responsibility. Just as Pharaoh was responsible for his actions and beliefs before God, so also are we. God does not want anyone to reject Him and His free offer of salvation (2 Peter 3:9; 1 John 1:9). But the choice is ours to make.

In his book *The Great Divorce,* C. S. Lewis stated that ultimately there are only two kinds of people: those who say to God, "Thy will be done," and those to whom God will say, "Thy will be done." The latter was the case with Pharaoh. He rebelled and persisted in his rebellion and sin so much that God gave him the desire of his heart—his own destruction.

TJD

7

AN UNNECESSARY LEGACY
~ ❈ ~

EXODUS 20:5

For I, the LORD your God, am a jealous
God, visiting the iniquity of the fathers
on the children, on the third and fourth
generations of those who hate me.

> ### How can the sins of one generation
> ### be passed on to another?

To hold innocent children responsible for the sins of their fathers is contrary to justice and fairness, and it seems an affront to the goodness of God. In fact, punishing one individual for the sins of another violates Scripture: "Fathers shall not be put to death for their sons, nor shall sons be put to death for their fathers; everyone shall be put to death for his own sin" (Deuteronomy 24:16; see also Job 19:4; Jeremiah 31:30; Ezekiel 18:20; Romans 14:4; Galatians 6:5).

But were the children innocent? The word *innocent* is often read into this passage or assumed. Note that the iniquity of the fathers goes on to the third and fourth generations (meaning simply future generations) of *"those who hate me."* That is, rather than being repulsed by sinful behavior in themselves and others, they find the very name of God repulsive and contemptuous. They have chosen to create and worship gods of their own making (idols, in violation of the second commandment) rather than the Lord God. Just as an apple tree produces apples, so rebellious parents produce rebellious children.

Scripture mentions the guilt of future generations in other contexts (Exodus 34:7-9; Leviticus 26:39; Numbers 14:18-19,33; Jeremiah 32:18-19). God longs to forgive a contrite spirit and, from a human perspective, is unreasonably patient with the obstinate and rebellious nature of people (Isaiah 48:9; Ezekiel 20:15-17; 1 Peter 3:20; 2 Peter 3:9). Judgment is God's very last resort. That's why Moses is able to call upon God's loving nature to seek and receive a reprieve from God on behalf of sinful Israel (Exodus 34:9; Numbers 14:19). The punishment that God brings on any generation is the result of its own injustice and guilt. These passages clearly show that judgment is exacted upon the guilty from generation to generation, never the innocent. Job provides appropriate words to those who would suggest that God punishes the innocent for the sins of their ancestors: "Let God repay him [the sinner] so that he may know it [what he has done wrong]. Let his own eyes see his decay, and let him drink of the wrath of the Almighty" (Job 21:19-20). God's wrath is for sinners, not saints.

Personal honesty in dealing with this passage will also serve us well. What nation, generation, or individual is innocent before God? Even the most faithful of generations, if it could be identified, is guilty before God and in need of repentance and a Savior who is willing to appease the justice of God with His own blood. That Savior of the Old and New Covenants is revealed as the Son of God, the Lord Jesus Christ of Nazareth: "There is salvation in no one else; for there is no other name under heaven that has been given among men by which we must be saved" (Acts 4:12). The penalty for sin is paid by the Son, not by saints. Praise God!

Absolute truth prevails in spite of the world's denial of it. Parents serve their children well by committing themselves to knowing and living the truth regardless of the effort required to accomplish this goal above all others. Parents can pass on to their children a knowledge of the Savior and of our need of Him. This is the best way to avoid unnecessary and unwanted judgment in generation after generation.

GPS

SHOW THEM NO MERCY

~ ❀ ~

DEUTERONOMY 7:2

When the LORD your God shall deliver them
before you, and you shall defeat them, then you
shall utterly destroy them. You shall make no
covenant with them and show no favor to them.

> **How could a good and loving God order the total**
> **destruction and genocide of Israel's enemies?**

God told the Israelites several times throughout their history to have no mercy on the enemy population in battle (Numbers 31:17; Deuteronomy 20:16-18; Joshua 11:20; 1 Samuel 15:18). Indeed, in Deuteronomy 7:2 the phrase "utterly destroy" carries the connotation of devoted destruction, a meticulous, intense, and intentional annihilation of the enemy.

With terms such as *genocide, holocaust,* and *ethnic cleansing* confronting us daily in the news in places such as Rwanda, Sudan, Kosovo, and Bosnia, how is this slaughter (which God commands) in the Old Testament any different? Surely a merciful and benevolent God wouldn't order such an action. And yet that is exactly what happened.

When we consider the destruction of the Canaanites and other peoples in the Old Testament, several considerations can give perspective (without mitigating or diminishing the events). Although God is patient (2 Peter 3:9), there are limits to what He permits from any person or people as He implements His plan for the world. A careful reading of the Old Testament shows that the dedicated destruction of

Israel's enemies, though total, was infrequent. It occurred because those nations violently and continuously opposed God's work and plan over a long period of time.

Although, like everyone, they deserved to die for their sins (Deuteronomy 9:4-5), God patiently waited for centuries to see if they would repent or if they would continue on their path of sinful self-destruction. The conquering Israelites themselves were not without sin, but the other nations' ongoing idolatry, immorality, and hatred of God was what brought about their deaths (Leviticus 18:25-30; Deuteronomy 7:10; 9:5-6).

The Canaanites had become like a moral cancer, and therefore just as a surgeon removes a tumor or gangrenous limb in order to save the body, so too did God order total war against Israel's enemies. God commanded this in order to prevent paganism from spiritually infecting the Israelites (Numbers 33:55; Joshua 23:12-13). Although God could just as easily have used nature or other means to accomplish His desires, He chose warfare. Though rarely noted, Jesus Christ will one day, at the end of the seven-year Tribulation after the rapture, conduct another war against the enemies of God that will make Israel's actions pale by comparison (2 Thessalonians 2:5-10; Revelation 19:11-21).

The command for acts of war such as those in the Old Testament does not apply to Christians (or anyone) today because God is not now working through one nation to establish His kingdom on earth. God commands no holy war, crusade, or jihad today. War is sometimes morally and ethically justifiable, but not on the basis of the verses cited above.

This passage and others like it demonstrate for us the destructive nature of sin and the ruthlessness that we should direct toward it in our own lives. Forgiveness is always available (1 John 1:9), but we should never underestimate the power of sin to detract us from God's plan and destroy our lives (1 Peter 5:8).

TJD

MASTER AND COMMANDER

~ ✻ ~

JOSHUA 5:14

No; rather I indeed come now as
captain of the host of the LORD.

> **Who is this person (Joshua 5:13) appearing**
> **to Joshua with his sword drawn at the**
> **outset of the battle for Jericho?**

Who is he who claims to be the captain (commander) of Jehovah's army? Was not Joshua given the honor of relieving Moses as commanding officer (Joshua 1:1-9)? What did Joshua see in this man that caused him to submit without hesitation and call him master and himself servant? Who could boldly request of Joshua that he remove his shoes while standing before him on holy ground (5:15)? Where else in Scripture can we find such words, and who is saying them?

The similarity of our passage with Exodus 3:2-6 helps to provide the answers to these questions. While Moses was tending his father-in-law's flock around Mount Sinai (Horeb), the Angel of the Lord appeared to him from the midst of a burning bush. Upon noticing Moses turning to look at the unconsumed fiery bush, the Angel of the Lord, identified as the Lord and God himself (Joshua 3:4,7), entreats Moses to "remove your sandals from your feet, for the place on which you are standing is holy ground" (3:5).

Other passages that describe the divine nature of the Angel of the Lord include Genesis 16:7-13 (He has authority to give life; see also 18:1-15); 48:3,15-16 (Jacob equates the angel with God); Exodus 23:20-23 (the angel forgives sin and has the name of God, which the Lord shares with no one but Himself—see Isaiah 42:8); Judges 2:1-4 (the angel claims to have made the same covenant with Israel as did the Lord; see Genesis 15:18); Judges 6:11-23 (the angel is called the Lord in verses 14-15 and performs a miracle in verse 21, and in verse 23 Gideon fears that seeing the angel will bring about his death); 13:16-18,20-23 (the angel's name is Wonderful, and Manoah fears that he and his wife will die because they "have seen God"); and Isaiah 63:8-9 (the angel is equated with the Lord as the people's Savior).

While Joshua was considering how to engage the Amorites at Jericho, a man appears to him and claims to be the commander of God's vast army. Joshua immediately falls prostrate before him and asks the commander for his orders. Joshua is not rebuked for this act of worship (see Revelation 19:9-10). The first order the commander gives is nearly identical to the Angel of the Lord's: "Remove your sandals from your feet, for the place where you are standing is holy" (Joshua 5:15). Then, in the following context (Joshua 6:1-5), the commander issuing the orders for a strategic plan of attack is identified as the Lord Himself. The "captain of the host of the Lord" and the Angel of the Lord are, in fact, one and the same: a theophany—God appearing in the form of a material being.

Which person of the Trinity most frequently interfaces with human beings on the earth? Since the Father's primary location seems to be in the heavens and the Holy Spirit works within the minds and hearts of people (Judges 13:6; 1 Samuel 16:14; Psalm 51:11; Ephesians 1:13; 4:30), it is not far-reaching to suggest that the Son of God who often and directly interfaces with humanity in the New Testament occasionally did so in the Old. Or would we suggest that the second person of the Trinity was mostly silent in the Old Testament while tremendously active in the New? No! The Angel of the Lord and the captain of the Lord's host is indeed the pre-incarnate Savior of the world, Jesus Christ!

GPS

10

WHY ME?

~ ❋ ~

JUDGES 6:13

O my lord, if the LORD is with us, why
then has all this happened to us?

Why do bad things happen if God is good?

These few words have been echoed throughout the eras of history. They are found here during the time of Gideon around 1200 BC, they were mentioned again in the middle of the fifth century BC by the distraught Judeans ("How have You loved us?" Malachi 1:2), and they are repeated today when people are frustrated with their circumstances or in despair. Actress Colleen Dewhurst, in the family classic *Anne of Green Gables,* aptly describes this attitude as "to turn your back on God." These words resurface across the airwaves after national tragedies such as public school shootings and the Islamic terrorist attack on 9-11. They take on a more secular and sinister nature when they question the very existence of God rather than simply question His willingness to intervene. Questions like this fail to take into account the reasons behind God's *apparent* lack of involvement in tragedy.

Calamity befalls human beings for at least four basic reasons. We will list three now and save the fourth for the end of this article.

1. *Creation versus people:* The created world is filled with risks, such as disease, accidents, and destructive weather.
2. *People versus people:* The world is inherently self-centered and prone to conflicts, including divorce and war.

3. *God versus people:* In our selfishness, we tend to minimize or exclude God. As we abandon our responsibilities and our relationship with God, we are left to our own inclinations and forfeit His guidance and protection.

Even though some risk of calamity lies squarely on the shoulders of human frailty and finiteness, still many wrongly believe that God should always ensure that they are not accountable for their own shortcomings or negatively affected by others' irresponsible behaviors. And when it comes to God holding us accountable for acting on our ever-present tendency to wander away from His protection or for our blatant disregard of His existence, we immediately become incensed and accusatory either to alleviate our guilt over rejecting Him or because He is not at our beck and call, acting in ways that we think are best.

The basic problem is that human beings apparently believe that God abandons or forsakes them for no legitimate cause, especially not for one that should result in some horrible calamity, whether as a result of divine judgment or happenstance. However, the truth is that humanity made the world threatening and unsafe by abandoning God. We are the wanderers, and He is the Way, but we despise direction. We are the obstinate children, and He is the responsible Parent, but we disdain discipline. We desire license, and He offers us truth, but we abhor absolutes. We are the problem and He is the solution, but we struggle against the need for a Savior. Our waywardness or selfishness creates our conflicts with creation, each other, and with God. Everything that we suffer, we suffer because we believe that God needs us, that God is not enough, or that we could somehow get along without Him.

The entire book of Judges depicts people wanting to live their own way (Judges 21:25) and, as a result, experiencing the consequences of life without God's guidance and protection. God is the one who appoints judges who will obey Him and redirect people back to Him. From the time of Adam's fall and throughout all of human history to this very day, God is the one who initiates relationships with human beings. God is doing the pursuing and persuading; we are responding. He came to us and continues to come to us so that we can come back to Him. Whether through judgment that comes directly from His hand (Isaiah 66:1-4) or through the judgment that is the natural consequence of our wanderings, God waits to receive back those who desire to return to Him and His protection. We want to be alone; He wants to be with us!

This is the essential question: Is God *with* those who are disobedient? Though we may assume so, He is not! Briefly look at Judges 6:12-13. In verse 12, the Angel of the Lord tells Gideon that God is with *him*. Gideon misses this crucial point and subsequently makes the false conclusion, "If the LORD is with us, why then has all this happened to us?" The point is that God is with Gideon, not with the people! We should keep in mind that God is not with those who abandon or rebel against Him. That is, He cannot be said to be on the same page with, in support of, or in agreement with those who oppose Him. He can still intervene in their lives or providentially control circumstances in their lives, but because of their disobedience or rejection, He is not with them.

Therefore, He either judges them directly or leaves them to the consequences of their choices, both of which result in calamity that He hopes will return the disobedient to obedience and fellowship. For example, if America wants God out of the public square, the consequence will be a democracy whose majority opinion will promote and defend behaviors that are consistent with God's absence (infidelity, divorce, abortion, euthanasia, and all the devaluing of life that accompanies such behavior—see Romans 1:22-32). Furthermore, if the nation decides that it wants God out of the public school system, it should not be surprised by the negative and sometimes violent behavior that fills the void created by the absence of God's influence. God is with the faithful; He abandons the unfaithful to their own devices, though thankfully never without some limitations or boundaries. In the end, God's plan for humanity will be realized, and those who abandon or reject Him will no longer have any influence in human affairs (Revelation 21–22).

What about the suffering of the faithful—those who remain in fellowship with God? We now come to the fourth cause of calamity.

4. *People versus God:* As the world rebels against God, it persecutes people who are reminders of its responsibility to God.

Though God does not abandon the faithful, they will because of their love for God experience the marginalization and extreme dislike of the world (Isaiah 66:5; John 15:18-27).

We know that "all who desire to live godly in Christ Jesus will be persecuted" (2 Timothy 3:12). And while we gain comfort from the fact that "God causes all things to work together for good to those who love God" (Romans 8:28), we do well to keep in mind that the "all things" refers to difficulties in this life, which include calamity, persecution, and even death. While the devil and his cohorts seek our undoing (1 Peter 5:8), God remains with us. Through every unfortunate circumstance we face, the Lord faithfully perfects, confirms, strengthens, and establishes us (1 Peter 5:10) for the sake of those who have yet to obtain the salvation which is in Christ Jesus (2 Timothy 2:10). Remaining steady on this path, the righteous find favor with God (1 Peter 2:19-20). Emmanuel—God is with us!

GPS

11
SACRIFICE OR SERVICE?
~ ❋ ~

JUDGES 11:31,39

Then it shall be that whatever comes out of the doors of my house to meet me when I return in peace from the sons of Ammon, it shall be the LORD's, and I will offer it up as a burnt offering. .. At the end of two months she [Jephthah's daughter] returned to her father, who did to her according to the vow which he had made.

Did Jephthah really sacrifice his daughter?

The biblical record in Judges 11:31-39 seems to indicate that Jephthah, a valiant Israelite warrior, made a vow to God that resulted in the sacrifice of his only child after he was victorious in battle against the Ammonites.

Some interpreters understand this passage to mean that Jephthah did not sacrifice his daughter but dedicated her to perpetual celibate service in the tabernacle. In this view, he offered her as a living sacrifice (in much the same sense that Paul says Christians are to be living sacrifices in Romans 12:1). This fits with the fact that Jephthah gave her two months (Judges 11:37-38) to lament not her impending death, but her permanent virginity, which she would keep as a servant in the national sanctuary. Her dedication meant not only that she would never marry and experience motherhood, but also that her family line would become extinct because she was an only child.

If she was sacrificed, why didn't God stop it as in the case of Abraham and Isaac? Also, God would not be likely to honor a vow that included killing a person. And Jephthah would not be likely to express his appreciation to God by committing an act contrary to God's Law.

Human sacrifice was expressly forbidden in the Bible and completely contrary to true worship (Leviticus 18:21; 20:2-5; Deuteronomy 12:31; 18:10). However, dedication for service was consistent with Old Testament practices and would also uphold Jephthah's inclusion in the list of heroes of the faith (Hebrews 11:32).

On the other hand, arguments for this being a human sacrifice and not a dedication are strengthened by the fact that the Hebrew word used in 11:31 points to a burnt offering. Although forbidden by God, human sacrifices did occur in Israel's history (2 Chronicles 28:3; 33:6).

The period of the judges was one of the low points in Israel's history. It was a time of moral and religious chaos (Judges 21:25). Jephthah was the son of a pagan prostitute (11:1-2). He may well have been influenced by the false religious practices (including those of the Ammonites, who practiced child sacrifice) that were so prevalent, and he may have consciously or unconsciously incorporated them into his own life (10:6).

Jephthah's words of lament in verse 35 seem to support a disastrous vow. The annual commemoration of the daughter in verse 40 also gives weight to the view that she was sacrificed. Although breaking a vow was a sin (Numbers 30:2), in this case, fulfilling the vow was a greater sin. Jephthah may have believed that God required him to fulfill his vow, but if so, he was badly and sadly mistaken.

Regardless of the view one takes, perhaps the greatest lesson of the story is the remarkable courage and character of the daughter, whose name we do not know. Regardless of her father's actions and beliefs, she remained steadfast, even in a personal tragedy.

TJD

A HOPELESS CASE?

~ ✳ ~

1 SAMUEL 3:14

*I have sworn to the house of Eli that the
iniquity of Eli's house shall not be atoned
for by sacrifice or offering forever.*

> **Can a person become so troublesome that God
> will prevent him or her from coming to faith?**

Though we may find the answer to this question disconcerting,
we must deal with the truth if we are to understand fallen humanity's
relationship with God correctly. Yes, God can harden the hearts of the
rebellious to such an extent that repentance is not possible. God decides
to whom He will and will not show mercy (Exodus 33:19; Joshua 11:20;
Romans 9:15; 11:25).

Eli's sons, Hophni and Phinehas, were priests who never understood the role they were to play among the people of Israel. Though
priests of the Lord Jehovah, they did not personally acknowledge His
authority (1 Samuel 2:12). Rather than handling the people's sacrifices
appropriately, they would take by force portions that belonged to the
Lord (2:15-16), thereby mocking the offerings to God (2:17). They also
practiced ritual prostitution, in the manner of their Canaanite neighbors,
in the environs of the tabernacle at Shiloh—a direct offense to God
(2:22-24; see also Deuteronomy 23:17). When their father heard of these
violations, his passive inquiry and concern fell on deaf ears. This mockery
of God's righteousness resulted in the divine hardening of Hophni's and
Phinehas's hearts (3:14), their deaths (2:34; 4:11), Eli's death (4:18), the

death of Eli's daughter-in-law during childbirth (4:19-20), the birth of a grandson whose name, Ichabod, appropriately marked the departing of God's glory from sinful Israel (4:20-22), and the eventual removal of Eli's house from the priesthood (2:27-30; 1 Kings 2:27,35).

Having mocked the sacrifice, Eli's sons removed themselves from its efficacy. God honored their choice of self-elimination by hardening their hearts to the grace of God, essentially leaving them in a state of condemnation. At a point known only to God, He decides to deny further opportunity for repentance. They had every opportunity to trust the revelation they had received and to honor God with faithfulness, but they chose their own path, which took them to their appointed end (Proverbs 12:15,26; 13:15; 14:12; see also God's dealings with Pharaoh in Exodus 3:19; 4:21).

Like Hophni and Phinehas, many people today *profess* to be believers, but for selfish reasons. They embrace it socially (for acceptance or control) and partially (in those areas with which they are comfortable or have agreement). Some are infatuated with the idea that faith is personal; they profess a "my god" theology—one that conforms God to human desire. One way in which this theology is manifested is in the belief that sincerity of faith is honored by God even when that sincerity does not include direct faith in Jesus Christ. This belief undermines the sacrificial nature of Christ's death; it taints the message of the Gospel, and therefore, has the potential of leaving its proponents, as well as others, without hope of salvation, as did Hophni and Phinehas's so-called sincere inculcation of Canaanite rituals into the Israelite system of worship. These folks know the truth of the Gospel, but for social acceptance and due to a false sense of compassion, they deny it. "If we go on sinning willfully after receiving the knowledge of the truth, there no longer remains a sacrifice for sins, but a certain terrifying expectation of judgment" (Hebrews 10:26-27).

GPS

13

THE UNFRIENDLY GHOST

~ ✳ ~

1 SAMUEL 16:14

*The Spirit of the L*ORD *departed from Saul, and
an evil spirit from the L*ORD *terrorized him.*

Did God send an evil spirit to terrorize Saul?

The presence of the Holy Spirit in the believer was different during the Old Testament period than it was in the New in one major way: In the Old Testament, the Spirit's presence in a person's life was temporary—there was no promise of permanent indwelling as is the case with believers in the New Testament. This explains the Holy Spirit's departure after Saul disobeyed the Lord. The Spirit's temporary indwelling was God's stamp of approval on Saul's kingship and the source of Saul's ability to envisage future events (1 Samuel 10:6,10), to exude courage (11:6), and to exercise popular influence (11:7). The Spirit of God gave Saul his ability and authority to represent God as the people's king, and Saul was a new man (10:6; see also 2 Corinthians 5:16-17).

Saul lost this ability and authority when he took upon himself the role of a priest (1 Samuel 13:11-14) and failed to obey the Lord's command to eliminate every residue of Amalekite life and economy (15:10-19). Rather than fearing the Lord (12:24-25), Saul feared the opinions and desires of his people, effectively allowing them to spare Agag, the Amalekite king, and the best of their sheep and oxen for, of all things, a sacrifice to the Lord (15:24). However, the Lord always prefers obedience over sacrifice (15:22-23). The consequence of Saul's disobedience was the departure of the Holy Spirit, which sealed the termination of his reign and initiated the arrival of a dogged evil spirit that would torment Saul to the day of his death (16:14,23; 18:10-12). His presence would bring Saul misery, fear, rage, murderous intent, and a grave depression.

The passage is clear; the problem, however, is found in the sensitivities of the interpreters. Why would a loving, gracious, and forgiving God send an evil spirit? A culturally acceptable or limited view of God's redemptive purpose, His authority, and His devotion to the truth for the sake of humanity too often prevents us from seeing and accepting God's absolute sovereignty, uncompromising holiness, and sole prerogative to deal with disobedience as He deems just. The Lord is thoroughly appalled by betrayal, completely intolerant of sin, and grossly offended by human arrogance, especially among those to whom much is given and from whom much is required. Saul and Ahab (see 1 Kings 22:20-22) were kings who bore the responsibility of preserving Israel's history and laws so that the nation would know peace and prosperity under the sole authority of their gracious and merciful God. Without these untainted laws and an accurate history, no sacrificial system remains to atone for the sins of the people. They would be lost to their own devices, wandering hopelessly into an eternal abyss, which is unacceptable to God because He is loving, gracious, and longing to forgive.

God is protective of His plan because truth, life, and the containment of the ravenous effects of sin are lost without it. Would you allow your children unsupervised visits with a grandparent whose lifestyle betrays decency and undermines the gospel? Hopefully not! Would you have the courage to keep your children away from such an influence, or would you be deterred for fear of offending the offender (see Deuteronomy 12:6-11; 1 Corinthians 5:1-6)? Leaders have a responsibility to ensure that truth and godliness are not sacrificed on the altar of tolerance. James warns teachers that their profession carries with it a greater judgment (James 3:1-2). Be willing to forgive repentant offenders of truth while never compromising it! Grace and toughness are not mutually exclusive. Fear and love of God is motivation enough to safeguard the truth (1 Timothy 6:20-21)!

GPS

14

DON'T FALL ON YOUR SWORD
~ ❋ ~

1 SAMUEL 31:4

So Saul took his sword and fell on it.

Is suicide a moral option?

The Bible records six instances of suicide. In none of the cases is the act accepted morally—the event is merely recorded. Those who commit suicide include Abimelech, son of Gideon (Judges 9:50-55), King Saul (1 Samuel 31:1-6), Saul's armor-bearer (1 Samuel 31:5), Ahithophel, advisor to David's son Absalom (2 Samuel 17:23), King Zimri (1 Kings 16:18), and Judas Iscariot (Matthew 27:3-10; Acts 1:18-19).

Advocates of suicide have suggested that Paul's longing to be with the Lord is a latent craving for suicide (Philippians 1:21-26). For believers, death does bring an end to personal suffering and begins total fellowship with God, but suicide harms others and prematurely ends faithful service to God and others. Paul loved God as well as the people with and to whom he ministered. He naturally desired to be with both. However, he rightly concluded that remaining in the flesh (alive) for the sake of the latter was more necessary.

Suicide is not the unpardonable sin, but like any believer's unrecognized sin, it does require a reckoning. Some attempt to add Samson to the list; however, his death is quite different. In an attempt to thwart the arrogance of a cruel enemy (Judges 16:23-25), Samson asks God to give him back his strength so that he can wipe out the leadership of the Philistines (Judges 16:26-30). He is not intending his death, but rather, as a warrior and leader of Israel, he is willing to sacrifice his life to cripple an enemy. This selfless and contrite act is not much different from many who, in the face of an enemy, sacrifice their own lives for others. We appropriately call these selfless feats "acts of courage," not suicides.

Many describe suicide as a "permanent solution to a temporary problem." Christians should take a second look at such a simplistic way to explain such an awful tragedy. Suicide is not permanent and solves nothing. Each person is created in the image of God and is therefore an immortal being with accountability beyond the grave (1 Corinthians 3:11-15; 2 Corinthians 5:6-10; Hebrews 9:27; 10:26-27). And from any perspective, suicide can hardly be seen as resulting from a single temporary problem. Suicide is a selfish and sinful action taken against oneself in order to eliminate what appears to be unrelenting and unaltering pain. It is the tragic and lethal culmination of a psychological process that converges unresolved events to create depression and hopelessness. People who end their own lives are burdened by many unresolved problems that are mostly, if not always, resolvable. Without help, unresolved burdens grow heavier until the weight becomes insufferable and the person is weakened to the point of despair. The future looks like their anxious past; hope to go on vanishes.

Habakkuk's response to the news that Jerusalem would be destroyed is insightful with regard to suicide. Though he is terrified at the thought of an invasion and fully understands the consequences of combat, rather than despair (turn his back on God), he places his trust, not in himself, but in the God of his salvation and strength (Habakkuk 3:16-19). The possibility of hunger and starvation are not enough to make him deny his God or his life.

Suicidal people don't want to die; they just don't know how to live. Habakkuk knew how to live! God is the mender of lives. Regardless of the circumstance, seek Him and you will find Him; trust Him and He will guide you; live for Him and you can know peace in the midst of tumult. A biblical understanding of God and of life inspires hope and diminishes despair. Choose God; choose life (Deuteronomy 30:19-20)!

GPS

CAUTION—HANDLE WITH CARE

~ ❀ ~

2 SAMUEL 6:6-7

*Uzzah reached out toward the ark of God
and took hold of it, for the oxen nearly upset
it. And the anger of the LORD burned against
Uzzah, and God struck him down there for his
irreverence; and he died there by the ark of God.*

> **Why did God kill Uzzah for trying to keep the ark
> of the covenant from falling off an oxcart?**

Perhaps you have heard the sarcastic quip, "No good deed goes unpunished." At first glance, that appears to be exactly what is transpiring in 2 Samuel 6:6-7. Uzzah was the son of an Israelite priest who was caring for the ark of the covenant, and God struck him dead when he touched the ark while trying to steady it during its transfer to Jerusalem during the reign of King David.

When David established Jerusalem as the political and religious capital of Israel, he sought to bring the ark of the covenant, the most significant and venerated item from Israel's past, to the city (1 Chronicles 13). For the Israelites, the ark symbolized the glory, blessing, presence, and power of God. It had previously been captured in battle from the Israelites by the Philistines in approximately 1050 BC and then returned after seven months (1 Samuel 4–6). Before and during its capture, the Israelites rebelled against God as their true leader and asked instead to have a king as their pagan neighbors and enemies did (1 Samuel 8:3-5). God permitted this but did not bless either the nation or Saul, the new king, and the ark was neglected for about 50 years. When David succeeded Saul, he wanted to revitalize the people physically and spiritually, and the 15-mile transfer of the ark was part of his plan for doing so. But David mishandled the ark, just as the Philistines had done shortly after its capture (1 Samuel 6:7-8).

When the ark was first constructed during Israel's 40 years in the wilderness, God commanded that it was never to be touched and was to be moved only by the Levite priests, who were to carry it on poles (Exodus 25:14-15; Numbers 4:15). David chose expediency over propriety in transporting the ark and Uzzah, the son of a priest who certainly knew better and whose name ironically means *strength*, participated in this corner-cutting activity and sin. David wanted to do things his way rather than God's way, and others followed him in this disobedience. But when God's Word is violated, the end does not justify the means. Good motives don't always produce desired results. The Philistines had improperly moved the ark too, but they did not have God's commands and were not held to the same standard, though they were still judged. Now, just as God had earlier struck down Israelites who presumptuously peered into the ark after its return (1 Samuel 6:19; see Numbers 4:20), so too was Uzzah killed for his sins of touching the ark, participating in its improper moving, and helping when he was not a Kohathite Levite (Numbers 4:15).

God considers any sin a serious matter. His instructions, commands, and words are not to be taken lightly or ignored. Uzzah did so, and his actions cost him his life—a high price for disobedience—and provided a clear lesson for everyone.

TJD

16

THE MORE THE MERRIER?

~ ❋ ~

2 SAMUEL 20:3

Then David came to his house in Jerusalem,
and the king took the ten women, the
concubines whom he had left to keep the
house, and placed them under guard.

Why does David have concubines?

A concubine is a woman who cohabitates with a man without being legally married, usually a slave woman in ancient societies who did not possess the rights of the free wife. David not only had many concubines, he also had many wives (2 Samuel 3:1-5; 5:13-16). This was the case with many of the ancients in the biblical record, including Abraham (Genesis 16:3), Nahor (22:24), Jacob (30:4), Eliphaz (36:12), Gideon (Judges 8:30-31), and Solomon, who had hundreds of wives and concubines (1 Kings 11:1-8).

Human nature is much more corrupt than we care to admit, especially as it relates to our passions, where we are extremely vulnerable and weak. In the area of marriage and sexual relations, these biblical characters too often reflect the culture of their time in the same way that many Christians today reflect their culture's sexual and marital mores. Christian participation in premarital sex and its growing tolerance of homosexuality is all too prevalent. The biblical characters of old violated God's standards, as many do today.

Some suggest that the Bible's lack of a prohibition on polygamy and concubinage amounts to an unspoken acceptance of these behaviors. The

Bible also fails to issue prohibitions on suicide and slavery, but they too are inappropriate. The point is that the lack of a legal prohibition is not the same as approval. In fact, the guiding principle for male and female relations makes prohibitions unnecessary—one man for one woman (Genesis 2:23-25). Furthermore, the prophet Malachi chides the people for being unfaithful to the "wife of your youth" (Malachi 2:14,16; note that he does not say, "the *wives* of your youth").

The idea that a person can divorce his wife to marry another violates a mutual agreement (Malachi 2:14), is offensive to the Holy Spirit (2:15), wearisome to the Lord (2:17), and ignores credible evidence against the acceptability of concubinage and polygamy. The vague reference to Abraham (2:15) most likely refers to Abraham having sexual relations with Hagar (Genesis 16:1-6), which is viewed in a negative light (see also Proverbs 31:3,10-31). Finally, Jesus Himself describes the original intent of marriage as an inseparable union between one man and one woman (Matthew 19:4-6,8-9; Mark 10:5-9; see also Romans 7:2; 1 Timothy 3:2,12; Hebrews 13:4).

The situation in 2 Samuel 20:3 is further evidence that multiple partners create problems. David's son Absalom had begun a futile rebellion to overthrow his father. Upon the advice of an advisor (2 Samuel 16:20-22), Absalom had sexual relations with David's concubines to convince the people that he had possession of all that belonged to David, thus successfully usurping the throne (see also 1 Kings 2:12-25). Upon returning to Jerusalem after repulsing the rebellion, David immediately had the ten concubines quarantined for the duration of their lives. They had become Absalom's possessions and therefore could no longer be sexual partners for the king. Though David provided for them, his failure to adopt God's view of marriage unnecessarily and negatively affected many lives. Such is also the case with Abraham, who fathered Ishmael, and Solomon, who loved the gods of his lovers and divided a kingdom (1 Kings 11:9-13).

GPS

TWO SCOOPS, PLEASE

~ ❋ ~

2 KINGS 2:9

Elijah said to Elisha, "Ask what I shall
do for you before I am taken from you."
And Elisha said, "Please, let a double
portion of your spirit be upon me!"

What is the "double portion of your spirit" Elisha desires?

The inheritance of a father was divided two thirds to the firstborn and a third to the remaining sons, so the eldest received a double portion of the father's wealth (Deuteronomy 21:17). With peace or fellowship offerings, meat was shared between the officiating priest, family members, and friends (Leviticus 3:1-17; 7:11-38). From the portion of the sacrifice that was given to Elkanah, a double portion was given to his beloved Hannah, and the rest was divided among his less favored wife, Peninah, and her children (1 Samuel 1:4-5). Elders of the church are said to be worthy of double remuneration (1 Timothy 5:17-18).

These examples refer to material assets. But is Elisha seeking a material opportunity by accepting Elijah's offer to be his successor (1 Kings 19:16-19)? Is Elisha being self-serving when he commits to stay by Elijah's side throughout Elijah's last day on earth (2 Kings 2:1-6)? Hardly! The fact is that Elijah had no inheritance to pass on to Elisha, except one—the mantle that he wore, which was a symbol of God's presence and power in him. What impressed Elisha was Elijah's commitment to God—his ministry. The hand of the Lord was on Elijah (1 Kings 18:46).

He predicted natural disasters (1 Kings 17:1-7), ensured God's blessing on those who assisted him (1 Kings 17:8-16), raised the dead (1 Kings 17:17-24), and stood up to the false prophets of Baal and to Ahab, the king of Israel (1 Kings 18:20-46; 21:17-26). And even though his ministry overwhelmed him at times, even to the point of hiding for fear of his life (1 Kings 19:1-14), still Elijah demonstrated an intimate and dynamic relationship with God for which Elisha longed.

A request for such a relationship with God was impossible for Elijah to grant. God alone could permit it. Was Elisha sincere enough, sensitive enough to God's leading? Was he willing to endure the difficulties associated with a life devoted to God? If Elisha was able to visibly witness Elijah's divine translation into the heavens, the Lord's answer would be yes (2 Kings 2:10). Elisha wanted to honor God with his life, receive enormous courage, and have innumerable opportunities to bring the message of God to wayward Israel. God knew Elisha's desire for ministry and granted him his request. He was to be Elijah's successor, as the prophets quickly witnessed by way of a miracle and the cynics quickly learned by way of judgment (2 Kings 2:15-25).

Think about possessing double the physical skills of Michael Jordan, twice the musical talents of Michael W. Smith, or the intellectual abilities of two Albert Einsteins. As great as these blessings would be, they are miniscule compared to having a double portion of God's Spirit working in our lives. For Christians today, the closest equivalent of this would be to desire a deeper relationship with the Holy Spirit (Ephesians 5:15-21), which involves setting self further aside. Yet we often fail to evaluate the depth of our desire to know and serve God without distraction (Hebrews 12:1). Imagine having a double portion of the apostles' desire to serve God publicly and confidently—to have double Augustine's desire to learn, Martin Luther's courage to strive for reform, or Jim Elliot's longing to see people know Christ as Savior. We each are equipped with spiritual gifts, but do we have the desire to let God use them completely and freely? "At night my soul longs for You, indeed, my spirit within me seeks You diligently" (Isaiah 26:9). "Whom have I in heaven but You? And besides You, I desire nothing on earth" (Psalm 73:25). More, more of God…and less, less of me!

GPS

18

BETHEL'S BAD BOYS
~ ❊ ~

2 KINGS 2:23-24

When he [Elisha] looked behind him and
saw them [the young lads], he cursed
them in the name of the LORD.

Why would Elisha curse "young lads"?

Unfortunate translations such as "little children" (KJV) and "small boys" (RSV) can lead to misunderstanding. Two nouns are used to describe the individuals who mocked God's prophet Elisha: *naar* (2 Kings 2:23) and *yeled* (2:24), both translated "lads." Both are broad words and can refer to infants, youths, or young adults. Context removes the confusion.

Jacob's 17-year-old son Joseph is called a youth (*naar*, Genesis 37:3), as are Eli's two sons, who are old enough to be priests (1 Samuel 2:12-17), and David's son Absalom, who is of marriageable age (2 Samuel 14:21,27; 18:5). Note, however, that Eli's sons and Absalom are "young" but willfully rebellious—youth does not equate to innocence. Daniel, Hananiah, Mishael, and Azariah were *yeled*, young men chosen by the king of Babylon for special training to serve in his court. To qualify for training, they had to be physically noticeable and possess superior intellect (Daniel 1:4,17). Both *naar* and *yeled* refer to young adolescents who are capable of all sorts of shenanigans but old enough to know better.

The young people confronting Elisha are of this sort—able to distinguish right from wrong. The town of Bethel, where these youngsters lived, is where Jereboam, Israel's first king after the division of Solomon's kingdom, established a center to worship Israel's new idols, complete

47

with a training center for priests (1 Kings 12:25-33). It is possible that all or many of these young men were priests-in-training. Having received what they might call dubious reports of the prophet Elijah's miraculous transport into heaven, they spot his successor on the road just outside of Bethel. As Elisha draws close, they begin to heckle him: "Hey, you old leper, why don't you go the way of Elijah and disappear!" The term "baldy" or "baldhead" is widely understood as a description for lepers who generally shaved their heads—they were considered outcasts with whom the elite had little patience. The youths didn't believe Elijah's message, and they certainly weren't going to accept the message of his successor. These hooligans were conveying their utter disapproval of Elisha, and by association, his God.

Note that Elisha does not face off with these hoodlums; he leaves their fate or judgment to God and moves on. The curse that he spoke was most likely well known by the people of Bethel but probably not taken seriously. "If then, you act with hostility against Me and are unwilling to obey Me, I will increase the plague on you seven times according to your sins. I will let loose among you the beasts of the field" (Leviticus 26:21-22). Bethel's "bad boys" believed a hybrid of the truth and paid the ultimate price as a result.

GPS

19

BURNING THE BONES

~ ✸ ~

2 CHRONICLES 34:5

*Then he [Josiah] burned the bones of the priests
on their altars and purged Judah and Jerusalem.*

What is the purpose of burning bones on an altar?

Idolatry is not something to take lightly. God abhors it, and the incident recorded in this verse shows how much it is to be avoided.

Josiah was the seventeenth king to reign in Judah, ruling from 640 to 609 BC after coming to the throne at the age of eight, following the assassination of his father. During his reign the "book of the law" (either Deuteronomy or the entire Pentateuch) was recovered during repairs to the temple (2 Kings 22:8-10; 2 Chronicles 34:8-18), spurring him to restore true worship in the land. Unlike most of his predecessors, he worshipped God and rejected idolatry and false religion, obliterating it in Judah. His actions and influence even went beyond Judah's boundary, extending into Naphtali to the north in Israel (2 Chronicles 34:6).

The restoration of biblical worship entailed more than tearing down and destroying idols and altars. It included opening the graves and exhuming the corpses of the pagan priests and then burning them on the altar at Bethel. Jeroboam I had erected this altar for false worship in about 931 BC (1 Kings 12:27-29).

The extreme action of burning the bones demonstrated the importance of not falling into idolatry. Josiah attempted to remove every trace of false worship and of those who led it. Burning the bones was a visible act that in effect said to the people, "because false priests offered false sacrifices, they too will have their remains burned on their altar, thus defiling it as a visible sign that God invalidates the sacrificial service they performed here."

According to the regulations of Leviticus, proper sacrifices to God included carefully carrying the ashes of sacrificed animals to a clean place for disposal. To do otherwise or leave them on an altar would defile it (Leviticus 1:16; 4:12, 6:10-11). In effect, every aspect of the rituals at Bethel was wrong even though the sacrifices had not been made to God. Josiah's burning of the bones is also recorded in 2 Kings 23:16.

Although the burning of the bones is an unusual event, even more remarkable is the fact that it is a fulfillment of prophecy. Two hundred and ninety years earlier, an unnamed prophet foretold this event, even stating that the person would be named Josiah who did it (1 Kings 13:1-2). God's prophetic words and plan are always fulfilled.

TJD

20

In God's Grip

~ ✲ ~

JOB 2:6

So the LORD said to Satan, "Behold, he
is in your power, only spare his life."

How can a loving God justify placing a faithful child into the hands of evil?

God's willingness to permit Satan to oppress Job caused Job unimaginable grief (Job 1:20-21) and immense personal discomfort (2:7-8,13). Satan compelled Job's enemies to attack and kill his servants and steal his working animals (1:13-15,17); he caused a ferocious lightning storm (which a witness mistakenly attributed to God) that burned his barns, killing the sheep and servants within and around them (1:16); he stirred up tumultuous winds that destroyed outbuildings, which collapsed on and killed his children (1:18-19); and, finally, he attacked Job's body with an agonizing skin disease. Though the onslaught against everything that Job loved and possessed was physically, emotionally, and mentally excruciating (3:1-26), he, unlike his wife, refused to swear at God or deny Him. He had been willing to accept the good from God, which was his in abundance, and initially, he accepted the adversity that befell him (2:10).

No one can deny that God allowed Satan to have his way with Job (with limitations). However, this does not make the Lord responsible for the evils that Satan carried out. "Far be it from God to do wickedness...to do wrong" (Job 34:10). Accountability lies squarely and only with Satan, in the same way nations (Assyria and Babylon) that God allowed to discipline Israel and Judah are held accountable for their actions (Isaiah

51

10:12-15; Habakkuk 1:6-11). Evil creatures always act consistently with their nature. We should be grateful that God keeps them at bay more often than He sets them loose.

Job was a righteous man (Job 1:1,8; 2:3) but certainly not a perfect man! Trying to grasp the cause of his troubles, he accused God of being indifferent (10:7), unresponsive (13:22-24), and unjust (19:6-7). Such behavior did not put God on an equal footing; it made Him appear inferior to Job, who was naively suggesting that he knew more than God. Pride was Job's unknown weakness. His wealth, position, and comforts had unconsciously created within him expectations that, under adversity, would reveal flaws for which, under the wise counsel of Elihu (33–37) and the Lord (38–41), he would be ashamed and from which he would turn (42:1-6). "God is greater than man.... He opens the ears of men, and seals their instruction [or "terrifies them with warnings," NET], that He may turn man aside from his conduct, and keep man from pride" (33:12,16-17).

Though Eliphaz wrongly suggests to Job that his calamity is the result of leading a wicked life, his understanding of God's intention to frustrate "the plotting of the shrewd, so that their hands cannot attain success" (5:12) is right on the money. God permitted Satan to pursue his evil intentions (1:9-12; 2:4-6) knowing that Job would endure and instruct Satan in the elasticity and durability of genuine faith—it may bend, but it never breaks when it is grounded in an uncompromising trust in God. In the end, the "helpless" Job was in God's grip, and Satan had to "shut his mouth" (5:16). As the Lord told Habakkuk, "The righteous will live by his faith" (Habakkuk 2:4), or as the New English Translation (notes 13–15) puts it, "The one who is innocent will be preserved by his integrity." Job was a man of integrity, and though his faith required pruning, he was destined to pass through the shears that cut him back so that he could grow stronger (Job 42:1-16) and learn, interestingly enough, not to assume a complete understanding of God's dealings with humanity. The same humility will serve us well when we are tempted to question God's ways.

GPS

21

DOWN BUT NOT OUT
~ ❋ ~

JOB 13:15

Though He slay me, I will hope in Him.

Why trust God if you think He is the source of your problems?

Job's three friends meant well. They were trying to comfort a person who was devastated by financial ruin, natural disaster, family death, and terrible health. The waves of suffering kept rolling in and crashing over Job, tossing him emotionally, physically, and spiritually against the rocks and shoals of despair.

Zophar, the third friend to try to comfort Job in his misery, bluntly tells him in chapter 11 that he is suffering because of his sins (something that was incorrect according to Job 1:1) and that he deserves what is happening to him. In chapters 12–14, Job replies as he did earlier with his friends Eliphaz and Bildad. In this response, Job makes his bold declaration in 13:15.

In this verse and the surrounding context, Job states that even if God slays him, he will still take his case of innocence before God and plead, as would a lawyer for acquittal. Job is affirming his faith in God and his innocence of sin: He would rather die proclaiming his innocence than continue to live under an assumed guilty verdict. Job was convinced he was innocent, and he was not afraid to be tried by God.

The exact way one of the Hebrew words in the verse should be translated is unclear and can lead to two renderings of the verse. One carries a foregone conclusion of death: "I have no hope." The second and more common translation gives the idea that even if death comes, Job will not relinquish trust in God: "I will trust regardless." Either the verse is one of despair or one of hope (as translated at the top of the page). Assuming it is taken as a statement of hope and confidence in the midst of suffering, it is indeed a remarkable pronouncement of faith, similar to his words in Job 1:21; 2:10; 19:25-26.

Three of Job's four friends offered advice that was well-intentioned but wrong. (Elihu was the exception in Job 32–37.) Job also had moments when his own thoughts were confused or incorrect. However, a thorough reading and study of Job shows a person who had a sincere, straightforward, and simple faith. Job's circumstances were complex, yet in the end, this man who probably lived around the time of Abraham understood that we live and die by the grace of God. Job also teaches us that we must live all of life by faith that God is good and aware of everything that happens to us—the good and the bad. Nothing happens to us that is beyond God's control and purposes even though we are not always aware of those purposes.

Two thousand years before the apostle Paul lived, Job endured enormous suffering. But in the end, he trusted God. Now, 2000 years after Paul's many adversities, we are living with struggles of our own. Just as Job's words in this passage were true for Paul (and us), so too do Paul's words for us resonate the same idea: "And we know that God causes all things to work together for good to those who love God, to those who are called according to His purpose" (Romans 8:28).

TJD

22

DRAGONS, DINOSAURS, AND DEATH

~ ✻ ~

JOB 41:1

Can you draw out Leviathan with a fishhook?

What kind of creature was Leviathan?

Two animals are mentioned in the book of Job that you probably will not find in the zoo—Behemoth (Job 40:15) and Leviathan (3:8; 41:1). Although many people have tentatively identified these with the hippopotamus and crocodile respectively because of similarities between those beasts and the descriptions in Job, neither of them probably corresponds exactly with any known animal in existence today.

Job was beset by enormous personal trauma and tragedies. In a brief span of time, he lost his health, his wealth, and his family. In the midst of his physical, spiritual, and emotional anguish, he cried out to God, seeking answers and explanations as to the purpose of his undeserved suffering. Job knew what it meant to wrestle with the problem of evil. And in the midst of Job's afflictions, God shows him that He often uses misery and suffering for purposes besides punishment. Among the several ways God demonstrates this are illustrations of 12 great and majestic beasts and birds over which Job has no control (Job 38–39). God then zooms in on two more creatures in chapters 40–41—Behemoth and Leviathan.

The word *Leviathan* is used six times in the Bible (Job 3:8; 41:1; Psalm 74:14; 104:26; Isaiah 27:1), but not every occurrence refers to the same creature. In Job 3:8; Psalm 74:14; and Isaiah 27:1, it is a natural sea monster or mythological creature. In Isaiah 27:1, where it is used twice, it is a symbol of the evil and fleeing enemies of God. But in Job 41:1, it is something different, and God's description of it is 34 verses long and very detailed.

Three explanations have been given for Leviathan's identification (as well as Behemoth's): 1) an unreal mythological monster, such as the seven-headed sea monster Lotan of Ugaritic mythology; 2) a real animal that exists today such as the whale, dolphin, or crocodile; or 3) a real but extinct creature such as a marine dinosaur that briefly survived Noah's flood.

If the creature in Job 41 were from pagan myths of the ancient Near East, then the whole argument of the chapter would collapse. The purpose of the chapter is for God to show Job that Job is not as wise as he thinks and that he foolishly charged God with being indifferent and inept. The context assumes it is as real a creature as the others. If Leviathan is a real animal, such as the crocodile, then the description does not completely fit even though there are many similarities (so also with Behemoth as a hippopotamus). That leaves the final option of a dinosaur-like water-living reptile known to Job and his era but not to us. This would then be one of the dinosaurs that lived before the great flood of Noah and perished in it or shortly thereafter, unable to adapt to a postdiluvian ecosystem.

The description of Leviathan in Job 41:1-34 certainly pictures it as terrifying, fearless, and peerless. Sparks of fire come out of its mouth (41:19), and no one can capture or subdue it. It is unlike anything else on earth (41:28-29,33). Nothing and no one are its equals. And that is exactly the point God is making to Job—hunters are unable to capture, kill, or destroy Leviathan, yet God controls it because He is sovereign. God, who controls the world and all that is in it, created both Job and Leviathan. God knew what He was doing in Job's life, even though Job did not—and God knows what He is doing in your life as well. Trust Him.

TJD

23

A FOUR-LETTER WORD

~ ❋ ~

PSALM 5:5

The boastful shall not stand before Your
eyes; You hate all who do iniquity.

Doesn't God hate the sin but love the sinner?

God loves the world so much that He gave His Son as a sacrifice for the world's treachery. However, He also hates the person who sins. God provided a way for sinful people to come into His sphere of incomparable love. He desires to love everyone, wanting no one to perish (Isaiah 48:9; 1 Peter 3:20; 2 Peter 3:9). Still, rebellious people continue to reject His love, placing them outside of divine love and making them subject to His holiness. When the unrepentant reject Christ's sacrifice for sin, God's hatred for sin has no other place to go but upon them. And yes, in that brief moment when Jesus became sin on humanity's behalf (Galatians 3:13; 2 Corinthians 5:21), fellowship between the Father and Son was severed as God placed His hatred of sin upon His Son out of love for us—amazing grace!

David's life as a believer was full of challenges, especially from enemies who pursued him and tried to take his life, including King Saul of Israel. Psalm 5 depicts David's weariness of dealing with external threats. He doesn't want these hindrances to interfere with God's divine purpose in his life, and so he prays in verse 8, "Make Your way straight before me." These pernicious obstacles have become so heavy on David's mind that he plans to make them the topic of his morning prayers (5:1-3), in which he uses a particular divine attribute or character trait (God's uncompromising holiness) to petition and hopefully persuade God to defend or vindicate him in the presence of his enemies (5:8).

David's description of God's attitude toward the wicked is unmistakable. God disapproves of evil, banishes the arrogant, hates those who behave wickedly, destroys liars, and despises violent and untrustworthy people (5:4-6). This attitude toward sinful people is not an isolated one. "The LORD tests the righteous and the wicked, and the one who loves violence His soul hates" (Psalm 11:5). "There are six things which the LORD hates, yes, seven which are an abomination to Him: haughty eyes, a lying tongue, and hands that shed innocent blood, a heart that devises wicked plans, feet that run rapidly to evil, a false witness who utters lies, and one who spreads strife among brothers" (Proverbs 6:16-19; see also Jeremiah 12:8; Hosea 9:15).

Biblical hatred is an attitude, not an emotion. It is a strong aversion to and rejection of evil, as the psalmist explains: "For Your lovingkindness is before my eyes, and I have walked in Your truth. I do not sit with deceitful men, nor will I go with pretenders. I hate the assembly of evildoers, and I will not sit with the wicked. I shall wash my hands in innocence, and I will go about Your altar, O LORD" (Psalm 26:3-6; see also Psalm 139:19-24). Hatred is repulsion and intolerance of and opposition to everything that is evil, anything that undermines good. What a person does not hate, he tolerates and eventually accepts as good (Isaiah 5:20; Malachi 2:17; Romans 1:32).

The problem with the phrase "God loves the sinner but hates the sin" is that it gives people a sense of false security. Because so many people believe that they are basically good and that God *always* loves them in spite of their "occasional" failings, they tend to take their waywardness (sinful acts) and God's amazing grace less seriously. Having known wickedness well and God's attitude about it (see also 5:9-10), David worships God for His mercy (or lovingkindness—5:7) and petitions Him for protection and blessing (5:11-12).

GPS

24

JESUS IS FOREVER
~ ❋ ~

PSALM 110:4

The LORD has sworn and he will not
change His mind, "you are a priest forever
according to the order of Melchizedek."

What is "a priest...according to the order of Melchizedek"?

This gentleman is somewhat of a mystery. The only personal information we have about Melchizedek is found in the space of three verses (Genesis 14:18-20). We next hear of Melchizedek 1000 years later (Psalm 110:4) and then again, after another 1000 years, by the author of Hebrews (5:10; 6:20; 7:1,10-11,15,17). He is briefly introduced, becomes a major piece in a messianic psalm, and finally is the focal point around which the superior status of Jesus Christ as King, Priest, and Savior is demonstrated.

People have tried to identify Melchizedek as Shem (the son of Noah), as an angel, or as a pre-incarnate manifestation of Jesus Christ. We should see him as the story itself does, so let's take a look. During a "border states" war, Abram learns that his nephew, Lot, is kidnapped. Abram determines to rescue Lot and return the stolen loot to its proper owners. After what we might call today a "strategic skirmish," Abram returns victoriously with Lot, numerous other captives, and the recovered plunder. The welcoming committee includes Melchizedek, the king of Salem and faithful priest of God Most High, who offers a blessing to Abram: "Blessed be Abram by the Most High God, Creator of heaven and earth. Worthy of praise is the Most High God, who delivered your enemies into your hand" (Genesis 14:19-20 NET). Out of admiration for this remarkable king, Abram gives him a tenth of all he repossessed. His name, Melchizedek, means "king of righteousness." He is king of Salem or "king of peace." He is a faithful priest of Jehovah as well as a king, and Abram's donation suggests that Melchizedek holds a superior position to him. Nothing more is said (see Hebrews 7:1-7).

In Psalm 110, David gives dominion not to himself, but to a future King, whom he calls, "my Lord." This King "sits at the right hand" of Jehovah, a position of supreme authority (110:1,5), and He will completely overcome and subjugate His enemies (110:1-3,5-7). But this King is more; He is also a permanent priest of the Melchizedek variety or type (110:4). Like Melchizedek, this Lord is therefore both a righteous *King* in pursuit of lasting peace—He will rid the world of His enemies—and a faithful *Priest* who is worthy of adoration. This is a new concept to David's readers—the functions of a king and priest were generally separate from one another. When the lines were crossed inappropriately, Saul lost his kingdom (1 Samuel 13:11-14), and Uzziah was stricken with leprosy (2 Chronicles 26:16-23). This King was unique. His reign would be without end, and as a Priest He would provide a sacrifice for the salvation of His people!

The writer of Hebrews brings Melchizedek and the Lord of Psalm 110 together in the person of Jesus Christ. There is no doubt that Melchizedek is a type of Christ; that is, he foreshadows, prefigures, or resembles the coming Messiah (Hebrews 5:5-6; 6:17-20; 7:11,15,17,21). Jesus the High Priest does not follow the Levitical order, which is temporal and incapable of stemming human waywardness (Hebrews 7:11-15; 8:8-9; 9:11-13). Jesus is from the order of Melchizedek, which is permanent (Hebrews 7:21-22,24) and capable of appeasing God's wrath and saving "forever those who draw near to God through Him, since He *always lives* to make intercession for them" (Hebrews 7:25; 8:10-13; 9:14-15; 10:11-14). What a King! What a Priest! What a Savior!

GPS

25

VERY HARSH WORDS

~ ❋ ~

PSALM 137:9

How blessed will be the one who seizes and
dashes your little ones against the rock.

Why is such a horrible action praised?

This is one of the harshest and most gruesome verses in the Bible, and certainly in Psalms. Why would the psalmist speak such words?

The poetry of Psalms vividly portrays the lives and struggles of its writers. The emotions in Psalms span the spectrum of human experiences. Each psalm also has a particular structure that falls into one of several categories, such as individual laments, national laments, praise and thanksgiving, and hymns of worship. Knowing what kind of psalm one is reading is a great benefit in studying the passage.

Psalms provides spiritual snapshots of the worship, thoughts, and prayers of the authors. Many of the psalms are very emotional and filled with images, symbols, figures of speech, and evocative language. Several of them, including Psalm 137, are known as *imprecatory psalms*. These invoke judgment or curses on the writer's enemies. In these prayers for punishment, the writers call on God to bring justice, punish evil, and vindicate the righteous. Imprecatory psalms are powerful portrayals of emotion and desire. Although very graphic, they are not personal vendettas. Rather, they are zealous prayers of longing that God would vindicate His causes on earth.

In Psalm 137, the author mourns the plight of Jews held captive in Babylon (see also Lamentations 1–2). In the first section (verses 1-6), he recalls how the exiles wept by the Euphrates River and its waterways as they mourned the destruction of Jerusalem. He vows never to forget Jerusalem, for it was not only home but also the center of Israelite worship.

The second part (verses 7-9) is a plea to God to punish the captors and their allies, the Edomites, who rejoiced in and encouraged Jerusalem's destruction (Ezekiel 25:12; Joel 3:19). The writer asks God to destroy the Babylonians, enacting upon them measure for measure that which the citizens of Jerusalem experienced.

The violent slaughter of infants and children portrayed in the verse was one of the barbarous practices of ancient Near Eastern warfare (2 Kings 8:12; Isaiah 13:16; Hosea 13:16; Nahum 3:10). It epitomized total warfare, effecting complete destruction of an enemy by destroying future generations. The Babylonians were famed for their cruelties, and the psalmist relishes the thought that someday they might experience a mirror defeat.

How does such a prayer of hatred correspond to other biblical teaching about love and charity? The Bible upholds the tension of the requirement for love and the hatred of evil. Indiscriminate hatred is wrong, and the psalmists, while writing out their own experiences, were also writing about the reality of evil under the inspiration of God. They prayed for divine retribution, looking to God for justice and the restoration of God's plan and reputation. Their prayers were not for personal gain.

Because Christians have both the Old and New Testaments, their prayer life is very different from the Old Testament saints'. Yet even prayers like "Thy kingdom come, Thy will be done," or "Come quickly, Lord Jesus," include an implicit prayer for the vindication of the righteous and God's judgment of evil. We are never to pray from passions that are selfish, vindictive, or judgmental (Galatians 5:15; James 4:13-16). Prayer is always a serious activity.

In *Reflections on the Psalms*, C.S. Lewis wrote, "The ferocious parts of the Psalms serve as a reminder that there is in the world such a thing as wickedness and that it (if not its perpetrators) is hateful to God." Prayer is one of the most serious and personal of the spiritual disciplines. Pray fervently, pray wisely.

TJD

26

FROM THE TOP DOWN

~ ❋ ~

PSALM 138:1

*I will give You thanks with all my heart; I
will sing praises to You before the gods.*

**Why would David talk of praising
God before other gods?**

The context of this verse clearly does away with the suggestion that
David has polytheistic leanings. David wants nothing more than to convince the nations around him (Psalm 138:4) that God alone is worthy of
adoration, the source of his thanksgiving, and the object of his undivided
praise (138:2). Whatever the gods are, they are not objects of worship.
For David, Jehovah's love and faithfulness are without equal (138:2,8).

The meaning of this phrase depends upon how the word *elohim* is
translated. Usually it is the word for God, but in some contexts, such as
this one, it takes on other meanings. At least four views have been proposed. The least favorable is that *elohim* refers to singing before the ark
of God. It seems odd that David would worship before the ark and then
immediately say, "I will bow down toward Your holy temple" (138:2). If
this view is correct, the two phrases are unnecessarily redundant or, at
least, should be reversed.

Others have suggested that *elohim* refers to an angelic assembly. The
intent of this psalm is to announce God's great love and faithfulness
to the nations—to convince them to join the writer in worship of his
magnificent Lord (110:4-5). Reference to singing before angels, in this
context, would be like "singing to the choir" or stating the obvious to

creatures who are already convinced. Though *elohim* can refer to angels ("heavenly beings"in the New English Translation of Psalm 8:5; see also Hebrews 2:7), a more widely used translation of the word is preferable in this context.

A third view proposes that the word "gods" refers to pagan idols. Their supposed abilities and powers pale before the greatness of Jehovah, whose word or promises are reliable; that is, they are as good as His name (110:2). Again, this is an acceptable translation, but David does not appear concerned with convincing the deities of anything. Rather he is interested in the worshippers of the gods and, probably more so, their leaders (110:4-5).

The fourth view seems to harness the most support. *Elohim* often refers to rulers and judges who, in a sense, are godlike in that they have been authorized by God to fill positions of power and represent His perspective in human affairs. "Moreover, he [Aaron] shall speak for you to the people; and he will be as a mouth for you and you [Moses] will be as God *[elohim]* to him" (Exodus 4:16). A slave appears before a judge *(elohim)* to remain with his owner (Exodus 21:6), an owner appears before a judge *(elohim)* to assess the effects of a theft, and rulers *(elohim)* are admonished for failing to stem injustice and care for the less fortunate (Psalm 82:1; see also 82:6; John 10:31-36). Rather than wanting to make his point before nonexistent gods, David vows to keep the truth and wonder of his amazing God before the ruling class, who in turn will influence their people. He does not shy away from presenting a clear and honest view of the supremacy of God, who is his strength (Psalm 110:3) and refuge (110:7). His hope is that neighboring rulers will take note of this great God and join him in singing praises to His matchless name. Engaging culture with enthusiasm over God's greatness and commonsense nature is every generation's responsibility. When the boss knows the Lord, influence among the ranks spreads. Does anyone really wonder why power is so important from Congress to the courts and from the White House to the workplace?

GPS

27

FEW AND FAR BETWEEN
~ ❊ ~

PROVERBS 18:24

*A man of too many friends comes to ruin, but
there is a friend who sticks closer than a brother.*

How can you have too many friends?

A person has friends for many reasons. Individuals who have great intellectual ability usually find themselves surrounded by aspiring students. Exceptional athletes have innumerable fans and journalists who long to bask in their glory. The wealthy tend to attract many friends because they have much to offer ("Wealth adds many friends...every man is a friend to him who gives gifts"—Proverbs 19:4,6). And people with similar interests vocationally or socially find it useful to befriend one another (two Marines in a foxhole certainly find each other's friendship indispensable). Generally, people with common human experience, interests, or direction are drawn together in friendship.

Friendship is generally a positive asset. Friends don't betray friends; friends don't let friends drive drunk. Friends protect, support, and care for one another! However, the word *friend* in Scripture is a bit broader. When used in a neutral or negative context, it speaks of a neighbor, companion, or simply another person, either placing little value on the friend or establishing a negative one. Those in the negative camp are pseudo or fair-weather friends (2 Samuel 16:15-17; Job 17:5; Proverbs 19:5-7; Luke 11:5-8; John 19:12). Those in the neutral camp are everyday friends or acquaintances with whom we interact socially and economically for the serenity and prosperity of the community (Jeremiah 3:4; Luke 5:20).

And finally, those in the positive camp are genuine friends on whom we depend in troubled times or adversity (John 11:11; John 15:13-15).

This loyal or genuine friend is clearly identified in the book of Proverbs. "A friend loves at all times" (17:17). "There is a friend who sticks closer than a brother" (18:24; see also 1 Samuel 18:1; John 15:13-14). A real friend will provide honest criticism rather than fear repercussions (27:6; 1 Kings 4:5). This friend doesn't leave your side when you mess up; he forgives you and stays with you through the consequences (Ecclesiastes 4:9-10). She never betrays confidences, even when doing so would profit her. Their commitment is based on unconditional love. They are there when you need them. Though fair-weather and everyday friends come in droves, the friends who become "closer than brothers" are relatively few. Their worth is incalculable.

Throughout our lives, we meet many people with whom we become friendly, both believers and unbelievers. These are the everyday acquaintances, and most, hopefully, will produce more good than harm. However, you must discern between those who genuinely love you and those who gain some advantage by having a relationship with you. Too many fair-weather friends might bring your life to ruin—this is the warning of our proverb! We are all selfish creatures and at different levels of spiritual maturity and understanding. How intimate believers get with other people will help or hinder the progress of faith. Here's the point: The best of friends should come from among the faithful, those who love and search out the mind of God in all matters. We can't manage many close friends—most of us are too busy—so choose wisely. Your faith and the faith of those you love depend on the quality of friends that surround you. Be friendly to everyone, but you cannot be everyone's friend!

GPS

28

THE THIN LINE

~ ※ ~

PROVERBS 21:14

A gift in secret subdues anger, and a
bribe in the bosom, strong wrath.

Does the Bible actually condone bribery?

The casual reading of the book of Proverbs can easily lead to misunderstanding. Often a proverb is nothing more than a statement of fact offered without any intent to moralize what is said. It doesn't always comment on the rightness or wrongness of a behavior. Such is the case here. A bribe that is given secretly ("in the bosom") subdues or soothes intense anger. The same is true of a secretly given gift. The proverb is a statement of fact—it can be true even if the truth is reprehensible. For example, "A bribe is a charm to the one who gives it; wherever he turns, he succeeds" (Proverbs 17:8 NIV). The meaning of the proverb is that bribers benefit from their bribes. This no more justifies bribery than the statement "For the lips of an adulteress drip honey and smoother than oil is her speech" (Proverbs 5:3) justifies adultery. The point of 21:14 is that both gifts and bribes have the same effect—they reduce anger in their receivers.

Gifts and bribes are different, the difference being determined by the giver's intent. A gift is a voluntary offering with nothing expected in return, as to honor a person. However, sometimes a gift is offered to soothe tensions and acquire desires. In Genesis 34, a man named Shechem was attracted to Dinah, Jacob's daughter, and sexually assaulted her. Hoping to restore trust with Jacob and receive his blessing to marry Dinah,

Shechem expresses his willingness to provide the family with a gift of their choosing. Though Jacob's sons used this genuine offer to unleash their fury against Shechem and his family, Shechem voluntarily offered the gift in hopes of soothing bad feelings and acquiring in marriage the woman he loved (Genesis 34:11-12). However, if Shechem's love for Dinah was nothing more than a ruse designed to avoid responsibility for his sexual misconduct, he offered a bribe disguised as a gift. Such is the reality of gifts—motives of a selfish nature quickly turn them into bribes. The thin line between gifts and bribes is drawn between just and unjust intentions (see Proverbs 18:16; 19:6).

The purpose of a bribe is to corrupt or control the behavior of the recipient. It's a payoff to persuade or induce a person to do something unjust or cover up an injustice for one's own benefit at the expense of others. The biblical position on bribes is unmistakable. "You shall not take a bribe, for a bribe blinds the clear-sighted and subverts the cause of the just" (Exodus 23:8; see also Deuteronomy 16:19). Bribery undermines justice by encouraging partiality for personal gain (Deuteronomy 10:17-18; 1 Samuel 8:3; 2 Chronicles 19:7; Proverbs 17:23; Ezekiel 22:12), it injures innocent neighbors (Deuteronomy 27:25; Psalm 15:5; 26:10; Isaiah 1:23; 5:23), and it is the tool of the unrighteous (Isaiah 33:15-16; Micah 3:11). A bribe's indicator is selfish intent or partiality, which makes justice its primary target, or enemy.

The difference between an anger-soothing gift and a bribe is the character of the person who offers or receives it. As Christians, we often walk a thin line between our old nature before Christ and our new nature in Christ (Ephesians 4:17-24). The side of the line we feed the most determines the appropriateness of the motives that shape our actions.

GPS

29

A LITTLE BIT MORE
~ ✹ ~

PROVERBS 27:20

Sheol and Abaddon are never satisfied,
nor are the eyes of man ever satisfied.

Where are Sheol and Abaddon, and
why are they never satisfied?

The book of Proverbs was written to provide instruction and wisdom for skillful and righteous living. It discusses almost every area of life and human relationships and gives timeless truths for all people and all cultures.

Proverbs 27 addresses issues of friends and relationships, offering its readers a concise manual on friendship and providing insights on the meaning of true friendship. Verses 17-20 include a series of couplets in which the first statement is a true fact of life that is then used as a simile for a social truth in the second statement. In verse 20 the first statement is one of the reality of death, and the second statement is about human desires. Just as death is an ever-present and increasing reality, so likewise is human greed. Such an appetite is reflected daily in consumerism, exploitation, and the desire for status.

Sheol and *Abaddon* occur together four times in the Old Testament. The Hebrew word S*heol* occurs 65 times and, depending on the context, is translated by terms such as *hell, pit,* and *grave.* It is usually a poetic word for the grave. It is also a place of punishment (Job 24:19) and horror (Psalm 30:9). Believers will be rescued from Sheol, but the wicked will not. *Abaddon* means "destruction" and occurs six times in the Old Testament and once in the New Testament, where it represents Satan (Revelation 9:11). In the Old Testament, it always refers to the destruction of the grave and a place of mystery and darkness.

In this verse, Sheol and Adaddon are personified as having a voracious appetite for devouring humans in much the same way that mythological monsters and pagan gods in the ancient Near East were portrayed. In the present age, everyone falls prey to death. Solomon's proverb reminds us that the same can happen with greed, tyranny, and the quest for power.

Someone once asked one of the robber barons of early twentieth-century America how much money it would take to satisfy his desire for wealth. Reportedly, the response was, "one more dime." That statement illustrates the principle of this verse. But it also invites a more positive response.

In 1 John 2:15-17, the apostle John reminded Christians that the desires and acquisitions of this world are temporary. They will not last. But salvation, the love of God, and eternal life will never fade away. "The world is passing away, and also its lusts; but the one who does the will of God abides forever" (1 John 2:17).

TJD

30

A Cake with Candles?

~ ☀ ~

ECCLESIASTES 7:1

A good name is better than a good
ointment, and the day of one's death is
better than the day of one's birth.

A valued friend eloquently and aptly described the day of his daughter's death: "This stinks." It was a day of loss and a day of tears; at times the grief was agonizing. A daughter, a sister, a wife, a mother, a special friend would no longer tease us, or we her. For the first time she was actually gone, and not just to another town to be seen at another time or called on a special occasion. She was gone, never to be heard from or touched in this life again! It was not a day of celebration—or was it?

Life is a tremendous challenge and often a tragedy. It is demanding and stressful, and human frailty and death abound. Sorrow is as much a part of life as is joy. Nonetheless, through sorrow we discover the depth of our faith and the convictions of our hearts. Struggle and sorrow can improve our lives (Ecclesiastes 7:2-3) and bring celebration.

At birth, I was totally dependent upon my family. I had no history; no one knew me. I had not become known for anything and knew nothing—no name or reputation (7:1). Growing up took me through the early years of innocence to the years of exploration and face-to-face with human selfishness—often exhibited by greed for power and position. The loss of friends to accident and suicide forced me to face mortality. More failures than successes have dotted the journey of my life, and disappointment of one kind or another will undoubtedly never be too far off (7:4). As my friend said, sometimes life really stinks. However, these struggles and sorrows helped me to see my greatest needs and forced me to commit to beliefs and values. I had to grow up and take responsibility for my actions. Sober reflection, rather than anger (7:9), should be the consequence of sorrow and suffering and the pathway to a more meaningful life (7:3; 1 Peter 1:6-9). This makes the "end of a matter...better than its beginning" (7:8).

In my seventeenth year, I accepted Christ as my Savior and Guide. This was the watershed moment of my life. From that moment to this, I have gained a greater knowledge of and appreciation for the Lord's person and purpose. There is no one and nothing that surpasses His greatness. He saved my soul, brought me into a deeper fellowship with Him (Hebrews 12:1-13), and gave me a greater appreciation of life, its challenges, and its wonder. Should Alzheimer's one day steal my memories, still God will remember me. I came into the world with nothing; I will leave it full of faith and spiritual wealth (Ephesians 2:4-10) and with an inheritance that is imperishable and waiting for me in heaven (1 Peter 1:3-5). He is the Alpha and Omega, the one who makes certain that the end of life is always better than its beginning.

David writes, "Precious in the sight of the LORD is the death of His godly ones" (Psalm 116:15). It pleases the Lord to see His children's struggles through life finally come to a close. His work of redemption in the believer is one step closer to completion (resurrection of the body remains), the cruel effects of sin are overcome, and fellowship in the presence of God is achieved. Acceptance of Christ as Savior makes what was uncertain at birth (salvation) a certainty at death. Faith identifies a person with the Lord, builds a solid name or reputation, and ensures that one's death will be better than the day of one's birth. In this sense, one's "death day," though painful, is also a celebration.

GPS

31

YOU WANT IT? YOU'VE GOT IT

~ ✻ ~

ISAIAH 28:13

So the word of the LORD to them will be,
"Order on order, order on order, line on
line, line on line, a little here, a little there,"
that they may go and stumble backward,
be broken, snared and taken captive.

What is the prophet really saying?

Isaiah 28–34 provides an extensive warning of judgment against the enemies of God. These chapters include a series of woes pronounced against the various groups that were opposing the words of the prophet Isaiah and God's message. These pronouncements were against rulers and people inside and outside the northern and southern kingdoms (Israel and Judah). Written between the years of 740 and 680 BC and at the time of the northern kingdom's conquest by the Assyrians in 722 BC, the book is an important historical record as well as a major book of prophecy.

In the first woe, a message to the northern kingdom (Israel) represented by Ephraim, its most prominent tribe, includes the confusing and almost nonsensical lines of the first half of Isaiah 28:13. They are also stated earlier in verse 10, and their repetition in verse 13 is a response to their usage in verse 10.

Verses 9 and 10 portray the prophets, priests, and leaders of Israel as being indignant at the words of Isaiah. They believed that he was lecturing them as if they were small children and with a condescending attitude (28:9). In verse 10, they mocked and mimicked his style. They were angry that Isaiah would treat them as little children.

The words "order on order, order on order, line on line, line on line, a little here, a little there" are a series of sounds in Hebrew. Much like we might hear someone say "yak, yak, yak, blah, blah, blah," the people uttered a string of sounds and words that expressed contempt for Isaiah and for God's message. They mocked Isaiah's prophecy as if they were children attempting to recite the alphabet.

The speakers did not intend the sounds of verse 10 to make sense. Perhaps because of their drunkenness (28:7), their hearing was impaired, and they only heard scattered syllables that they repeated in derision, or perhaps they were mocking as if they were speaking baby-talk or gibberish.

In verse 11, Isaiah responds and tells them God's message will come through foreigners. The main sin of the people was their unbelief in God's Word and their lack of faith in Him. Therefore they would be judged not through the words of a prophet, but through an invading army that would be the physical manifestation and fulfillment of the prophecy of woe that they mocked. It is as if God said, "If you don't want to hear 'blah, blah, blah,' then I will show you 'blah, blah, blah' in the form of an invading army."

God's communication, whether written or spoken, is never to be taken lightly. This passage is a strong reminder of the truth that "God is not mocked" (Galatians 6:7).

TJD

32

YOUR LIFE MATTERS

~ ✳ ~

JEREMIAH 1:5

Before I formed you in the womb I knew you,
and before you were born I consecrated you.

> **How important is each human life, and when**
> **does God consider a human being valuable?**

Each and every one of us longs to be loved and desires a sense of security. The reason we should love each other and provide each other with safety is simple: The unlimited value that God places on each of us demands nothing less.

The second phrase in the verse, "before you were born I consecrated you," usually gets the most attention because it clearly gives unlimited value to each human life prior to its birth. It is appropriately used by pro-life advocates to defend the personhood of the baby before its experience outside of the womb. In the mother's womb, God consecrates (sets apart or chooses) each of us for a particular purpose within His will, which we discover through obedience or diminish through disobedience.

As important as the second phrase is to placing value on human life, the first phrase is even more compelling. When I made my entrance onto the stage of life in my mother's womb, He already knew me. In fact, He made it possible for me to even be in the womb at all. Before we existed in human form, our lives existed in the mind of God. "Before I formed you in the womb, I knew you." Talk about someone thinking about you—we were in God's thoughts before we were in our parents' thoughts. Talk about purpose—God wanted me to live before my parents did! He had a plan for me before there was a "me."

But someone might say, "Jeremiah was brought into existence to be a prophet—he was a specific choice for a specific purpose. We all are not so fortunate. The value placed on human beings is therefore limited to specific persons—not every person born is of equal value." It certainly is possible to argue that this passage has specific reference to Jeremiah and could be extended to others like him. For example, David, speaking of himself, says that the eyes of God "have seen my unformed substance; and in Your book were all written the days that were ordained for me, when as yet there was not one of them" (Psalm 139:16). However, New Testament passages clearly show that the importance and unlimited value of human life is applied to all.

Clearly, God's desire is that each member of the human race accept His Son as his or her Savior and become a member of the body of Christ (1 Corinthians 6:15; 2 Peter 3:9). And as a member of the body of Christ, each person plays a critical role in the body's life and influence. Whether a person is in a pastoral position, an elder, a staff member, a teacher, or a maintenance worker, he or she provides the impulse that makes the body run smoothly. If any part of the body fails, the entire body is affected, and its life and influence is diminished. "The body is not one member, but many" (1 Corinthians 12:14).

You and I entered the mind of God, the wombs of our mothers, and the world to make a difference—for God first and foremost and then for others. Regardless of what one's religion might now be, each of us was formed in the mind and by the hand of God to be obedient to and used by God for His glory and our good. If we alter His original intentions for our lives, we alter our ability to glorify Him and honor and protect ourselves. Only through obedience to God do we fully realize the real value of our lives and our desire for love and security. Make a difference—love and obey—your life matters!

GPS

WASTED EFFORT

~ ❀ ~

JEREMIAH 7:18

The women knead dough to make
cakes for the queen of heaven;
and they pour out drink offerings to
other gods in order to spite Me.

Who is the queen of heaven?

The very first commandment written by God on the tablets of stone that Moses brought down from Mount Sinai was, "You shall have no other gods before Me" (Exodus 20:3). Idolatry in any form has always been forbidden. And yet it persisted throughout the history of the Israelites and remains a major spiritual problem throughout the world. Much of today's spirituality and religion is simple idolatry. Perhaps its prevalence throughout history is part of the reason for the priority of its prohibition in the Ten Commandments.

The reference to the "queen of heaven" in Jeremiah 7:18 is one of the many biblical references to idols. The verse occurs in a sermon given by the prophet Jeremiah (7:1–8:3) at one of the seven gates to the temple court in Jerusalem about 608 BC. In his message of judgment to the southern kingdom, Judah (the nation Israel divided into the northern kingdom [Israel] and the southern kingdom [Judah] following King Solomon's death in 931 BC), Jeremiah denounces the idolatry and false religious practices of Judah's inhabitants. The people believed that judgment would not come to Jerusalem because it was the site of the temple. Yet the people weren't using it as a talisman and a source of protection. They believed that regardless of their pagan practices or spiritual hypocrisy, they would be safe from invasion or judgment. But God declared through Jeremiah that He would not tolerate their idolatry.

God cites one example of Judah's idolatrous worship, stating that throughout the nation people were kneading dough to make cakes for the queen of heaven. They were preparing food offerings for an idol. The cakes were actually formed in the image of the idol (Jeremiah 44:19) and then offered along with wine. "The queen of heaven" refers to Ishtar, the Babylonian goddess of love and fertility. Ishtar was one of the many false deities in Mesopotamia, Canaan, and Egypt and was known throughout the area specifically as the "queen of heaven" or the "mistress of heaven."

Idolatry in any form or any age is a rejection of God's sovereignty and power. Idolaters abandon the biblical worldview and faith in God in favor of a futile and frivolous object or idea. The practice of idolatry in Judah was not something new for God's people. According to Amos 5:6, the Israelites had a long history of slipping into idolatry, even carrying idols with them during their 40-year wanderings in the wilderness after God delivered them from slavery in Egypt. Wherever the Israelites lived, idolatry was an issue.

Israel's history of idolatry carries a lesson for each of us: We are never exempt from temptation. Theologian Carl F.H. Henry astutely observed, "The pagan option is always knocking at the door of the person who crowds God out of his or her life."

TJD

34

SOMETHING OLD, SOMETHING NEW

~ ❁ ~

JEREMIAH 31:22

*How long will you go here and
there, O faithless daughter?
For the LORD has created a new thing in the
earth—a woman will encompass a man.*

> **What does it mean for a woman to encompass
> a man, and when does it happen?**

"Something old, something new, something borrowed, something blue." So goes the saying for brides and what they carry on their wedding day. Is this passage also about romance and relationships? It is certainly speaking about something new for someone. This unusual verse is one of the most perplexing verses in Jeremiah. Throughout the centuries, the exact meaning has eluded interpreters, who have offered several views on precisely what this prophecy means. No single interpretation has gained a majority understanding.

The verse occurs in the midst of two important prophetic chapters (30–31) regarding the restoration of Israel and Judah, the two halves of the nation of Israel that split several hundred years before Jeremiah wrote (627–585 BC). With the nation in captivity, chapter 31 tells of a future restoration. Verses 1-22 concern the northern kingdom (Israel), verses 23-26 refer to the southern kingdom (Judah), and verses 27-40 apply to both kingdoms. The restoration of which Jeremiah prophesies is a yet future time that will occur after the seven-year Tribulation. It is then that both the northern and southern kingdoms will be fully restored to their land (Amos 9:14). It does not refer to the nation's return in 616 BC, which was only a partial return.

Jeremiah looks beyond the immediate circumstances to a future restoration, when Israel will receive the blessing of a new covenant (Jeremiah 31:31-34). The future will be dramatically different from the misery and suffering of Jeremiah's day.

In verse 21, God tells Israel to set up markers and guideposts (as was the custom of caravans and travelers) as they traveled into captivity in Babylon so they could return once God permitted their restoration. When this happens (verse 22), something new occurs—a woman will encompass or surround a man.

An old but unlikely view coming from the early church fathers is that "a woman encompassing a man" is a prophecy of the virgin birth of Jesus Christ. It understands the "new thing" that is created as the incarnation of Jesus. But this does not at all fit with the context, and the verb "encompass" has no sense of conceiving.

Others see in the verse the idea of protection so that during this time things will be so peaceful that those who are physically (or perhaps militarily) weaker will be able to protect a stronger partner. Within this view is the possibility that it means that women will be able to protect the nation Israel or even that Israel, like a woman, will overpower her enemies.

Some find in this unique prophecy a reversal of what was then the cultural custom of the male initiating the courting of a woman. While such a practice may very well occur, a wider meaning than social mores is probably in view here. Closer to the context is a view that understands the woman to refer to Israel and the man to be God, with Israel returning spiritually to God. Just as God has throughout history embraced and loved Israel, so in the millennium will Israel fully embrace and love God.

Although specifics regarding the verse are uncertain, what is certain is that Jeremiah is saying something amazing and hard to believe will occur for the nation Israel in the future. As with all of God's dealings, it will be wonderful, exciting, and majestic. It will surpass anything experienced thus far on earth.

TJD

35

THE HIGH PRICE OF IDOLATRY

~ ✦ ~

EZEKIEL 20:25

I also gave them statutes that were not good
and ordinances by which they could not live.

Did God really issue bad laws?

This bewildering declaration by God, given through the prophet
Ezekiel to Israelites from the southern kingdom (Judah) being held in
captivity in Babylon, occurred between 593 BC and 571 BC, the dates of
Ezekiel's ministry.

Ezekiel's prophecy reminded the exiles of the national sins that had
caused their judgment, and it assured them that God had not forgotten
them and had a future plan for them. As part of his prophecy, Ezekiel
gave a sermon about rebellion and restoration. In this review of Israel's
history of disobedience to and defiance of God (Ezekiel 20:1-44), especially during the 40-year wilderness journey after leaving Egypt (near
1440 BC), God speaks of laws that Israel could not keep.

Two generations of Israelites participated in the wilderness sojourn—
those who came out of Egypt and those who were born after the
departure. Ezekiel 20:10-17 talks about the idolatry and disobedience
of the first generation, and verses 18-26 speak of the second generation's
idolatry. Both generations practiced idolatry, and both received temporal
judgment. Part of the judgment of the second generation was letting their
sins run the full course in their lives.

Some interpreters have wanted to identify the laws in verse 25 with
the Mosaic Law, including the Ten Commandments. However, such an

interpretation contradicts other biblical passages that speak of the Law as good and an expression of God's righteousness (Romans 7:12,16). Also, the Mosaic Law was given to the first generation coming from Egypt (Ezekiel 20:11), and in this passage Ezekiel is speaking about the second generation.

The statutes and ordinances verse 25 refers to are the laws and practices of the pagan nations that Israel adopted. These were not laws that God gave but laws that Israel chose over God's Law. Thus God "gave Israel up" to its own desires. Such laws included human sacrifice (20:26), something God specifically prohibited (Leviticus 18:21; 20:1-5). The sacrifices spoken of here were probably to the Ammonite god Molech (1 Kings 11:7; 2 Kings 23:10), to whom infants were sacrificed in a fire. In their practice of false religion and idol worship, the Israelites were rebelling against God, who let them temporarily go their own way. But the practices were also the judgment (similar to what Paul describes of others in Romans 1:24-28). God simply allowed their sins to run their full course so that the Israelites experienced the consequences of their choices. The sin of the Israelites became its own punishment (Psalm 81:12). Idolatry always was (and is) a senseless and fatal attraction.

TJD

36

ALL IN THE FAMILY
~ ✳ ~

HOSEA 1:2

Go, take to yourself a wife of harlotry,
and have children of harlotry.

Why would God command His prophet
Hosea to marry a prostitute?

Did God ask Hosea to commit an unsuitable, if not sinful deed? We know that *priests* were explicitly told not to marry prostitutes, but they were also not allowed to marry divorced women (Leviticus 21:7), which was permissible for others (Deuteronomy 24:2). A priest's responsibility as an intermediary between penitents and God demands a stricter lifestyle (Leviticus 27:2). Additionally, the apostle Paul makes clear that a sexual union with a prostitute is indeed immoral (note that Paul is not referring to marriage). The body was created to be in fellowship with the Lord and used in His service, not used for selfish sexual gratification (1 Corinthians 6:15-18). Was Hosea marrying a temple prostitute to satisfy his sexual pleasure, or was he marrying her to perform a service for the Lord?

Though marriage to a prostitute would certainly lift more than a few eyebrows and would indeed be a violation of proper association between believers and unbelievers (Ezra 10), Hosea's marriage to Gomer was different for the simple reason that God directed it. Unlike every person before and after Hosea, he was not lured into a sexual relationship with a godless woman for sensual or selfish reasons; he was obeying the Lord. He did not sin—when he slept with her, she was his wife. He entered the relationship with his eyes wide open, knowing that his soon to be troubled marriage would ultimately bring glory to God—the people of Israel would see their spiritual condition through the voice of the prophet and the vivid imagery of his family.

Hosea's marriage was an illustration of God's marriage with Israel. Hosea approaches Gomer with an offer of marriage. As a pagan temple prostitute, she may have been delighted and grateful that someone would see any value in her. Given the comparison between her and Israel, she may have taken pleasure in this new opportunity, this gift of freedom. Initially the marriage was good (2:15), but the honeymoon would not last long. Hosea represented a loving husband who was willing to forget the past to create a prosperous future. He wanted the most for his wife and family and was willing to put his character on the line for love, but his love was not enough. Though rescued from bondage and loved more than she had ever been, Gomer returns to her former loves (2:5).

Like Hosea, God knew what He was getting into. He made a contract (a covenant) with a people who were in dire need of His guidance and care. They were a sinful, cantankerous bunch who often saw God as a ticket from hard times rather than a promise of better times (from Egypt to the Promised Land). Still, He entered into a marriage, willing to abide by the agreed-upon covenant. However, they forgot who rescued them, and they credited their prosperity and power to other gods and devoted themselves to them (2:5,8; 4:1,10,18). Rather than rest in the God who loved them, they slept with gods who lured them, and they became an adulterous nation.

Faithfulness is all in the family—Hosea's, God's, mine, and yours. If we are to love Him, we must never forget how much He loved us (see Hosea 10:12; 11:1-4,8-9) and what He went through to secure our salvation (Hosea 13:4-5; Isaiah 53:3-6; Philippians 2:7-8; Hebrews 12:2-3). The family of God is a bride preparing herself for marriage with the Son of God. May our track record during this time of betrothal show our sincere and pure devotion to Him alone (2 Corinthians 11:2-3; Revelation 19:7).

GPS

37

HERE, THERE, AND EVERYWHERE

~ ❁ ~

HABAKKUK 3:3

*God comes from Teman, and the
Holy One from Mount Paran.*

> **If God is everywhere, how could He come
> from Teman, and who is the Holy One?**

One of the many characteristics or attributes of God is His omnipresence—the fact that He is everywhere at once with His whole being. At all times, His presence is everywhere in His entirety (Psalm 139:7-11). Though God may act differently in different places (that is, He may punish, sustain, or bless), He does not have size or spatial dimensions and cannot be contained by any space or place (1 Kings 8:27). *Omnipresence* does not mean that parts of God are spread throughout the universe or that God is one with the universe (pantheism).

Habakkuk's prophetic book, which he wrote in 607 BC, concerned God's plan to punish Judah by sending them into captivity in Babylon. This prophecy came true in 605 BC when Nebuchadnezzar invaded Judah and deported the prisoners (including Daniel) back to Babylon. The book culminates in the last chapter, and that is where the present verse is found. It is a prayer and lengthy psalm of praise, extolling the person and power of God.

In verse 3 Habakkuk recounts the magnificent deeds and miracles God performed when He brought His people out of Egypt, through the wilderness, and into the Promised Land. As Habakkuk recounts the history of God's people, he is reassured that God will also one day deliver them from their coming captivity in Babylon.

A careful reading and understanding of the historical background of verse 3 shows that Habakkuk is talking about God's works in the past and not His character or attributes. Teman was a desert oasis and region in southern Edom (the land occupied by Esau's descendents and called Seir in Genesis). It was the region between the Dead Sea and the Gulf of Aqabah flowing into the Red Sea and was part of the area of the Israelites' 40-year wilderness wandering. "The Holy One" is a reference to God (Habakkuk 1:12). The precise location of Mount Paran is not known but like Edom, it was part of the wilderness region and located to the southeast of Israel in the Sinai area. From here Moses sent spies into the land of Canaan (Numbers 13:3,6). The song of Moses (Deuteronomy 33:2) also mentions Mt. Paran.

In what sense did God come from these places? From Habakkuk's perspective, God did so by being with the children of Israel throughout their desert sojourn as illustrated by His presence with them at these two locations. Habakkuk is saying that just as God was with His people throughout the adversity and judgment of the exodus, so too would He be with them as they experienced the next time of judgment and adversity in Babylon.

Habakkuk 3:3 is a good illustration of the practicality of theology. Too frequently it is misconstrued as something worthy only of debates and academic tomes. But that is a misunderstanding. By its nature and content, theology is always relevant. In this instance, an insight regarding the person and presence of God throughout the adversity of His followers reminds us that regardless of our own circumstances, God is with us.

TJD

38

IT'S IN THE CONTRACT

~ ✳ ~

MALACHI 1:2-3

I have loved Jacob; but I have hated Esau,
and I have made his mountains a desolation
and appointed his inheritance for
the jackals of the wilderness.

How can a loving God hate Esau?

The prophet Malachi was a person of few words. In a style of questions and answers in an intensely personal conversation between friends, he reminds listeners of God's covenant faithfulness to Israel and rebukes them for disobeying and neglecting God. Affirming God's love for them, Malachi begins with very powerful words about Jacob and Esau. Later, in Romans 9:13, Paul cites these same words to teach the doctrine of election.

The account of Jacob and Esau in Genesis describes one of the most famous sibling rivalries in the Bible. But it is also an illustration of God choosing, before the creation of the world, some people to receive salvation. Election assures that the chosen will receive salvation, but it does not save them. They must still have faith in the substitutionary death of Jesus Christ on the cross. Every person has the responsibility to accept Jesus Christ.

Election is one of the hardest concepts in the Bible to understand, and for many, to accept. However, it is taught repeatedly (Romans 8:28-30; 9:11-13; Ephesians 1:4,12; 2 Thessalonians 2:13; 2 Timothy 2:10; Revelation 17:8). It is simply an act of differentiation wherein God chooses certain people for certain purposes (in this context, salvation). It is a choice grounded in God's love and grace. It is unconditional and not based upon anything God sees or knows that makes an individual worthy of choosing.

Several biblical and theological concepts, such as foreknowledge, predestination, and reprobation, are associated with election. Each of these is a significant part of the larger doctrine of salvation. Just as a person might speak of the legislative aspect of government, but a broader discussion would include the judicial and executive branches, so also are all the concepts above separate but related.

The words "love" and "hate" in Malachi 1:2-3 involve the technical language of legal documents and covenants in the ancient Near East. In the Bible, God specifically uses legal language and forms in His promise to Abraham of a posterity and land (Genesis 12:1-3; 15:1-5,18-21; 17:1-8). God reaffirmed the promise to Isaac and Jacob, and now, to Malachi's listeners, who were direct recipients in this line of blessing. The words "love" and "hate" may carry emotional overtones in this context, but they are fundamentally ideas of a social and legal nature.

Jacob received the birthright, inheritance, and blessing of the family line and covenant (though he obtained it through ruse and deceit). God accepted Jacob according to the covenant, and He rejected Esau. And because the Israelites were Jacob's heirs, God reaffirmed His acceptance and love for them through Malachi's writing. Even though Jacob's descendants were unfaithful, God was perpetually faithful to His contract that accepted one brother and rejected the other. Jacob's descendants survived conquest and captivity, but Esau's did not. In His sovereignty, God chose one to accomplish His plan, and in so doing, the other was legally rejected.

The Bible portrays election as a comfort, a reason to praise God, and an incentive for evangelism (Romans 8:28-30; Ephesians 1:5-6,12; 1 Thessalonians 1:2,4; 2 Timothy 2:10). It is not fatalistic and must always be seen in the larger context of God's love for the world and desire that every person repent and ask for salvation (2 Peter 3:9). That includes you.

TJD

39

HEY, NOBODY'S PERFECT

~ ※ ~

MATTHEW 5:48

You are to be perfect, as your
heavenly Father is perfect.

Can humans be perfect?

When Jesus spoke these words, He was definitely setting a high standard for anyone wanting to be a disciple. Is Jesus really commanding perfection, and does that mean it is possible?

Jesus repeatedly taught that all humans are sinful (Matthew 22:18; Mark 7:21-22; Luke 7:37-48; John 8:34). No person is without sin. It is a universal condition and problem, and everyone needs salvation (Romans 3:23; 6:23). In fact, the Bible clearly teaches in 1 John 1:8 that if people (and specifically Christians, to whom this short letter was addressed) claim to be sinless or perfect, they are liars. The sin nature is in everyone, even Christians, in whom it periodically erupts like a volcano (Ephesians 2:3). Yet Christians are to live ethically, imitating Jesus Christ in all their actions, knowing that after death or Christ's return, they will receive a glorified resurrection body like His (Galatians 5:16-25; 1 John 3:2-3).

Jesus' words about perfection are found in the context of what is known as the "law of love," and the focus is not about sin, but love (Matthew 5:43-48). In Jesus' day, the religious leaders taught that people had a higher moral and ethical obligation to their neighbors and family than to strangers (Leviticus 19:18). Jesus now tells His followers that their obligation is broader; it is to all people. Just as God permits the sun to shine on everyone and sends life-giving rain on the good as well as the evil, so too should Christians not be selective in their ethical behavior toward others. Jesus illustrated this very principle with the story of the Good Samaritan (Luke 10:29-37). In every aspect of our lives we should strive to do the right thing—what Jesus would do.

Jesus' declaration to be perfect is similar to His words in Luke 6:36, "Be merciful, just as your Father is merciful." Acts of mercy and kindness are not to have restrictions on them, for that is what God is like. In our ethics and behavior, we are to be equal-opportunity practitioners, acting without social, racial, gender, or cultural discrimination. God doesn't discriminate, and neither should we.

TJD

40
SHOW SOME DISCRETION
~ ✳ ~

MATTHEW 7:1
Do not judge so that you will not be judged.

Isn't judging people sometimes necessary?

Many people don't want to criticize or be criticized, but the fact is that judgment has its proper place. To understand its place, we must first recognize two kinds of judgment: discernment and sentencing. The former is appropriate within guidelines, and the latter is out of bounds.

Discernment demands theological and biblical prudence, and since we all are maturing in these areas, we should never be too quick to comment on the behavior of others. People who discern must be careful to express God's convictions on a given issue or behavior rather than opine from the standpoint of their own sensitivities or proclivities. Simply stated, we must be certain that when we speak, we speak for God. In so doing, the judgment, criticism, or assessment must not be our own, but rather a confident and humble reflection of God's authority, given for the benefit of the one addressed (see James 2:12-13).

Too often spirituality is assessed by how long someone has been a Christian rather than how Christlike a person has become. To call out someone else's misconduct when such misconduct mirrors our own is inappropriate and hypocritical. What God requires in you, He also requires in me. The entire world will be judged by one standard, and it is not of human origin (Matthew 7:2-3). So rather than judging as hypocrites (as people with logs in our eyes, trying to remove the specks in others'), our discernment should serve the common good (see Romans

12:9-10; 1 Corinthians 12:7) by being consistent with God's standard of behavior.

Discernment should be exercised only when it might produce a positive effect. "Do not throw your pearls before swine" (Matthew 7:6). Just as Jesus would not perform miracles to satisfy Herod's musings (Luke 23:8-9), we should not offer character evaluations of people who seek only to mock and belittle God's treasures. Discernment is not about a person having greater spirituality than another or being more able or qualified to critique. It is about a body of forgiven saints who choose to work together to create an environment where each is encouraged to pursue the likeness of Christ for the benefit of the whole (1 Corinthians 12:20-25) and to reflect that likeness to the world, which has yet to grasp the significance of God's amazing grace.

Discernment is one thing; sentencing is another. A person can discuss misconduct, but judgments that condemn personalities are presumptuous and out of bounds. No human being will give counsel to God during the Great White Throne judgment. God will have no jury. Unfortunate statements such as, "If you do that, God will condemn you to hell," or "You have committed the unpardonable sin and are condemned forever," or "If you keep that up, God will bring great calamity into your life" are without foundation and arrogant, and they usurp God's authority and prerogative. None of us is worthy of the blood that gives forgiveness and life, and none of us knows who will respond to God's grace or how God will work in the hearts of others. Therefore, no one can assume that the worst among us are beyond His grace (see James 4:12).

GPS

41

TRUE CONFESSIONS

~ ❈ ~

MATTHEW 10:32-33

Everyone therefore who shall confess Me
before men, I will also confess him before
My Father who is in heaven. But whoever
shall deny Me before man, I will also deny
him before My Father who is in heaven.

> **What does it mean to be denied by Jesus, and**
> **when does He deny those who deny Him?**

Discipleship carries with it a grave responsibility; it is not to be entered into without serious contemplation. Being a Christian involves service, commitment, risk assessment, and unconditional devotion or loyalty to Jesus Christ. Discipleship requires humility (Matthew 10:24) and unwavering trust in God's sovereignty over one's life. It includes loving Him above all others and all things (10:35-37). It is more than a personal or private faith that exists between the believer and his Lord; it is a public faith that unashamedly testifies to the truth and person of Jesus Christ, who is Lord and Savior of all (Romans 1:16-17).

Knowing that discipleship can be intimidating, Jesus gives His followers three reasons to preach the gospel with confidence: 1) Nothing that the wicked do goes unnoticed by God (Matthew 10:27-29; Luke 12:1-3); 2) the enemies of God kill the body, but God has the authority to take life and condemn the soul forever (Matthew 10:28; Luke 12:4-5); and 3) God's intimate knowledge of the least of things ensures that He will not forget the faithfulness of His children (Matthew 10:29-31;

Luke 12:6-7). Do not fear people; fear God, who never forsakes His own (Genesis 28:15; Deuteronomy 31:6,8; John 14:1-3,18-19; Hebrews 13:5). He will never renege on the promise of eternal salvation, which He promises to those who trust in Christ. Those who openly confess their loyalty to Jesus Christ can rest assured that Jesus will openly acknowledge such loyalty to God, the Father. On the other hand, Jesus will disown or refuse to acknowledge to His Father anyone who chooses to repudiate or renounce loyalty to Him (Matthew 10:32-33; Luke 12:8-9).

What do people confess and deny? Earlier in this chapter, Jesus tells His disciples that many in Israel have denied His claims of kingship and divinity by calling Him Beelzebub, a name for Satan, the prince of demons (10:25). After warning His followers of the cost of discipleship (10:16-23) and exhorting them to fear God above men (10:26-31), Jesus then makes a statement regarding their response to His claims: Acknowledge My claims, and I will acknowledge you; deny them, and I will deny you. After His ascension (Acts 1:6-11), Jesus will take His place at the right hand of the Father as Judge (Luke 22:69; Acts 10:42-43; 17:30-31). Though His denial of those who deny Him is perpetual, final judgment will happen at the Great White Throne and lead to the second death (Revelation 20:6,11-15; 2 Peter 3:7).

Nevertheless, we must continue to engage culture with the gospel of Christ secure in our confession and confident that all people will one day bow before Jesus, either as King through confession or as Judge through denial (Philippians 2:10).

GPS

42

BLASPHEMY AGAINST THE HOLY SPIRIT

~ ✳ ~

MATTHEW 12:31

I say to you, any sin and blasphemy
shall be forgiven people, but blasphemy
against the Spirit shall not be forgiven.

What is blasphemy against the Holy Spirit,
and why did Jesus say it isn't forgiven?

These are among the most enigmatic and emphatic words Jesus speaks in the New Testament. His words in this verse (also in Mark 3:28-30 and Luke 12:10) certainly raised the eyebrows of the religious leaders, the Pharisees, to whom He was speaking. Many people since then have also wondered about this unforgivable sin. In the Gospel of Mark's account of this much-debated saying, Jesus declares that blasphemy against the Holy Spirit is not only unforgivable, it is also eternal.

When Jesus spoke of this unpardonable sin, He had been confronted by the Pharisees, who condemned Him for healing a man who was blind, unable to speak, and demon possessed. The Pharisees accused Jesus of being under the power and influence of Satan, mockingly called Beelzebul after an Old Testament pagan deity (2 Kings 1:2). In response to these charges, Jesus utters the words regarding blaspheming the third divine person of the Trinity, the Holy Spirit.

To blaspheme is to slander someone. In the Bible, to blaspheme was to insult or demean the person, name, or character of God. Rather than honoring God, a person guilty of blasphemy cursed or reviled God and His name through derogatory words and actions.

When the Pharisees tied Jesus' actions to Satan, they were rejecting Jesus as Messiah and on the brink of making an irreversible decision with far-reaching consequences: They would never find national or individual salvation and forgiveness. Because they incorrectly attributed to Satan the power of the Holy Spirit that Jesus exercised in His miracles, they blasphemed the Holy Spirit. The religious establishment of Jesus' day misidentified divine actions as demonic actions and rejected the person and work of Jesus Christ as Messiah and Savior. Because Jesus was physically present when the rejection occurred, some interpreters of this verse hold that blasphemy against the Holy Spirit cannot occur today, although rejection of the Spirit's work is certainly possible.

In this passage (Matthew 12:32), Jesus states that a specific or single act of blasphemy against Himself, the Son of Man, can be forgiven. Speaking out against Jesus and His ministry is subject to forgiveness because such words or acts of rejection come from misunderstanding the reality of His person and work. However, once the Holy Spirit works in people's lives, convicting and convincing them of the truth of the gospel (John 16:8-11) or correcting misunderstandings about Jesus, a subsequent persistent and decisive rejection of the Holy Spirit's work regarding Jesus results in permanent judgment. Persistent obstinacy leads to permanent condemnation.

Jesus tells His listeners that all blasphemies can be forgiven except this one against the Holy Spirit because it demonstrates in attitudes, actions, beliefs, and practices a defiant hostility toward God. It does so by rejecting God's offer of salvation expressed through the power of the Holy Spirit and manifested in the words and work of Jesus. Although the Pharisees had been exposed to Jesus, the Light of Truth (John 3:19), they permanently rejected Him, preferring spiritual darkness to light. In so doing, they blasphemed. In rejecting Jesus, the Pharisees and others, though apparently being convicted by the Holy Spirit that Jesus was indeed the Messiah, refused to believe and rejected God's only means of salvation (John 14:6). An unrepentant heart leads to an unforgivable heart. Present choices have eternal consequences. What a person believes about Jesus and His death on the cross has eternal significance. Accepting Jesus is the greatest decision we make in life.

TJD

MATTHEW 16:20

Then He warned the disciples that they
should tell no one that He was the Christ.

> **Why would Jesus instruct His disciples**
> **not to tell others that He was, in fact, the**
> **promised Messiah, the Christ and Son of**
> **God (see also Mark 8:30; Luke 9:21)?**

Elsewhere in the Gospels, Jesus demands that people not reveal His identity or His wondrous works of healing. After cleansing a leper, He admonishes him not to tell others, but to go to the priest to make the appropriate sacrifice (Matthew 8:4; Luke 5:14). He strictly told the two blind men He healed not to discuss their healings with others, a command which they promptly ignored (Matthew 9:30). After healing a man with a withered hand as well as numerous others among the crowd and being publicly identified by unclean spirits to be the Son of God, He warns the people, and quite possibly the unclean spirits, not to make His works and identity known (12:16; Mark 3:12). He expressly tells Peter, James, and John not to talk about His wondrous transfiguration, the appearance of Moses and Elijah, or God's audible voice, which expressed great pleasure in His Son, until after His resurrection (Matthew 17:9; see Luke 9:36). And finally, He categorically stipulated that no one in the multitude who was witness to the resurrection of Jairus' daughter discuss the miracle publicly (Mark 5:43).

Note that all these demands for silence closely follow healings and the disciples' startling realization that they were in the company of the Messiah—God's anointed one! As people heard Jesus teach and experienced His power over physical ailments, the crowds grew larger and the demands for His "skills" grew greater. People love heroes; they love to put them in power as protectors or national icons. For the most part, these people were not looking for a suffering servant or a savior from sin (Isaiah 53; John 6:15); they wanted a savior from Roman rule, a charismatic leader—a messiah of their own making.

Misrepresentations of Jesus were plentiful (John 7:40-53). Some thought of Him as an intriguing and inspiring teacher; some saw Him as a ticket to good health (Matthew 11:20-24; John 12:17-19) or food (John 6:26); others saw Him as one more great Jewish prophet or another John the Baptist, Elijah, or Jeremiah (Matthew 16:14); the Pharisees saw Him as a fake, an impostor, and worthy of death (Matthew 12:14; John 12:9-11); but a few had their mind opened to the fact that they were indeed in the presence of divine majesty (Matthew 16:17). This unique King was not seeking a crown; He was seeking a cross through which He would offer salvation from sin to the entire world (Matthew 12:18,21; Isaiah 42:1,4; see Genesis 22:15-18). However, at this time, a path of suffering and death would not be favorable to the multitudes (John 12:27-41) any more than it was agreeable to the disciples (Matthew 16:22; Mark 9:30-32; Luke 24:18-21). For the time being, they wanted Him to live; He needed to die!

Jesus knew how selfish and shortsighted people are. In time, the attitudes of the multitude would change with the urging of their leaders. Many of those He healed would eventually look upon Him with hate. He knew that once the Pharisees, Sadducees, and rulers in the synagogues fully comprehended His claim to divinity and the Messianic throne, they would accuse Him of blasphemy against God and treachery against Caesar. At His choosing, Jesus would officially disclose His divine identity and purpose before the Sanhedrin (Matthew 16:21; 26:63-64; Luke 9:22). Until then, and fully aware of human fickleness (John 2:24-25), He occasionally asked the crowds and His disciples not to make His works or true identity known. Jesus was controlling the timing of His death (John 2:4; 12:23-36)!

GPS

44

RETURN OF THE GREAT PROPHET

~ ❋ ~

MATTHEW 17:11

*He answered and said, "Elijah is
coming and will restore all things."*

Why did Jesus say Elijah was going to return?

Elijah was considered one of the greatest of the Old Testament prophets. He and Enoch were the only two people in the Old Testament who were taken to heaven without dying. Elijah was the one who prophesied that there would be a three-year drought in the land during the reign of King Ahab (1 Kings 17:1; James 5:17). He was also the one who challenged the false prophets and priests of Baal, calling down fire from heaven on Mount Carmel (1 Kings 18:1-46). And Elijah was the one who, without dying, was miraculously carried to heaven by a chariot and horses of fire (2 Kings 2:11). Four hundred years later, the prophet Malachi declared that someday, before "the great and terrible day of the LORD," Elijah would return (Malachi 4:5-6).

Belief in Elijah's return was therefore a normal expectation in Jesus' day, and so some people thought John the Baptist was Elijah who had returned. Both Isaiah (40:3-4) and Malachi (3:1) predicted the coming of a forerunner, and Jesus declared concerning John the Baptist that "if you are willing to accept it, John himself is Elijah who was to come" (Matthew 11:14). If Israel had accepted Jesus as the Messiah at His first coming, John would have fulfilled the prophecies regarding Elijah. But the Jews rejected Jesus, so the prophecy will yet be fulfilled as one part of God's prophetic plan (Acts 3:21). In fact, when John the Baptist was asked directly, "Are you Elijah?" he declared, "I am not" (John 1:21).

With this background, in Matthew 17:11 Jesus declared to His disciples that Elijah would one day return. And He made this statement immediately following the appearance of Elijah and Moses in splendor along with Himself on the Mount of Transfiguration (Matthew 17:1-5). Peter, James, and John were confused by this event. They had just seen a glimpse of heaven and of Jesus in His glory with Moses and Elijah standing next to Him. They were confused about Elijah and asked for more information. Jesus then reaffirms to them that Elijah will yet return.

Elijah's return is a yet future event. One common interpretation holds that a likely time of fulfillment of this prophecy is during the first part of the seven-year Tribulation (after the rapture). Revelation 11:3-13 describes the ministry of two unique people who will proclaim the gospel for 1260 days during the first part of the Tribulation. Referred to simply as the "two witnesses," these individuals will be clothed in sackcloth, a symbol of doom and repentance (Isaiah 37:1-2; Daniel 9:3). The two witnesses are usually identified as Elijah and Moses.

The ministry of the two witnesses will include preaching, prophesying, and performing miracles. They will call people to repentance, and they will encourage faithfulness to God regardless of circumstances. Until their ministry is completed, God will protect them from those who seek to do them harm. Eventually, the Antichrist will kill them, but God will physically resurrect them after three and a half days and take them to heaven in a cloud.

The prophecies of the Bible are always fulfilled. Jesus told the disciples that Elijah would one day return, and this is only one part of God's prophetic plan. It is a reminder to each of us that we are not to take lightly God's words and Word.

TJD

45

TOUCHED BY AN ANGEL

~ ✵ ~

MATTHEW 18:10

See that you do not despise
one of these little ones,
for I say to you that their angels
in heaven continually
behold the face of My Father who is in heaven.

Does every child have a guardian angel?

The spirit world is very real. The presence and work of angels (and demons or fallen angels) were recorded throughout the Bible. Angels were present at creation, sang at Jesus' birth, and warned Joseph and Mary to flee to Egypt. Angels ministered to Jesus during His 40 days in the wilderness. They were present at Jesus' tomb after the resurrection, they witnessed His ascension, and they will be present at the rapture and the second coming.

Jesus also taught about angels. He mentioned them in Matthew 18, where He told the disciples that they needed faith marked by humility and childlike traits of trust and an eagerness to learn (18:1-5).

Who are the "little ones" of whom Jesus was speaking in verse 10? One view is that they are children like the one who stood with Jesus as He taught this passage (18:2). A second view is that "little ones" refers not to children, but to believers in Jesus Christ who in their faith and actions display characteristics *like* the child with Jesus. In this view, the words "one such child" earlier in verse 5 refers to Christians rather than children.

The first view would make Matthew 18:10 a passage about children and guardian angels. However, regrettably, it teaches very little about them. And nowhere else does the Bible contain any suggestion of one angel for one person—adult or child. We are simply left with this verse to affirm their existence, and further questions must remain unanswered. In this view, Jesus may be saying simply that angels protecting children have perpetual access to God's presence.

The second view would make the verse about Christians and angels and not specifically children. It could mean that some or all Christians (children and adults) have guardian angels or angels who minister to them at specific times. Such ministry may be continual, as in the assignment of a guardian angel, or it may be a brief ministry to individuals at particular times similar to the ministry of the angel Gabriel to Zechariah (Luke 1:11-20) and to Mary (Luke 1:26-38).

One variation of the latter view is that the word "angel" refers not to angelic beings, but to the spirits or souls of believers after death, who are in the eternal presence of God. This view (held by theologian B.B. Warfield), requires an unusual but not impossible interpretation of "angel" in 18:10. Elsewhere, Jesus taught that Christians in heaven are "like" the angels in certain aspects (Matthew 22:30; Luke 20:36) though always greater than and separate from them. They are similar but separate. Although not a strong argument lexically, it is possible.

Yes, this verse could possibly teach that guardian angels exist for some children, if not all. We know that angels exist and at times, God sends angels for protection (Psalm 91:11-12). Children and adults may have guardian angels. If they do, because of the Bible's silence, anything else on the topic is speculation rather than substance. The Bible tells us all we need to know for a mature and growing relationship with God; it does not tell us all we want to know. Scripture is sufficient, but it is not exhaustive (2 Timothy 3:15-17).

TJD

46

WHAT'S IN A NAME?

~ ✵ ~

MATTHEW 23:9

Do not call anyone on earth your father;
for One is your Father, He who is in heaven.

Is it wrong to call a parent or someone else *father*?

Many cultures, religious traditions, and individuals show respect for elders or specific leaders by addressing them with the title *father* or some other familial form. Indeed, the Bible commands people to honor and pray for not only their parents, but all of those who have some type of authority over us, familial or otherwise (Exodus 20:12; 1 Timothy 2:1-2; 1 Peter 2:17). What then does Jesus mean when He tells His disciples and a listening crowd not to use the word *father* for anyone but God?

This command by Jesus comes in the context of a larger warning to His listeners regarding the hypocrisy and unbelief of Israel's religious leaders (Matthew 22:1–23:8). Jesus told them that the desire for positions of honor and respect and accompanying titles such as *rabbi, father, teacher,* and *master* were not to be sought for their own sake or taken lightly. Israel's religious leaders had an enormous responsibility to accurately teach, interpret, and practice the Word of God. But they were not doing so. Instead they were using their positions for their own gain and self-esteem. They were misinterpreting Scripture and yet expecting absolute allegiance. Their practices were similar to those of many religious leaders and false teachers today. Jesus is telling His listeners and disciples that they are not to be spiritually arrogant and hypocritical. Just as they were not to argue about who would be greatest in the future kingdom of God, neither were they to abuse their role as disciples and spiritual leaders (Matthew 18:1-4). Humility rather than self-exaltation is the characteristic of true disciples.

Because the context of this verse is dealing with religious leaders of Jesus' day and their use and abuse of titles, Jesus is not talking about biological fatherhood. Nor is He talking about spiritual fatherhood in the sense that Paul was a spiritual father to his young protégé Timothy (1 Corinthians 4:15; 2 Timothy 1:2). Rather, Jesus is telling His audience that God alone is to be exalted, venerated, and given unquestioned loyalty and obedience.

TJD

47

THE BEGINNING OF THE END

~ ✳ ~

MATTHEW 24:34

Truly I say to you, this generation will not
pass away until all these things take place.

> **To whom was Jesus referring when He**
> **talked about "this generation"?**

Some say "this generation" refers to the disciples, but no one who was alive when Jesus spoke those words ever saw the return of Christ. Who then is "this generation," and to what "things" was Jesus referring?

This verse occurs in a major passage of prophecy (Matthew 24–25; see also Mark 13 and Luke 21) known as the Olivet Discourse. Jesus' sermon in these two chapters is His longest prophetic sermon and one of the most important prophetic texts in the Bible. These verses have also, not unexpectedly, been among the most controversial as people have sought to interpret them—and controversy usually brings confusion!

Some people have thought that the generation Jesus referred to is connected to the mention of the fig tree two verses earlier in Matthew 24:32, and that the fig tree is a symbol for the reconstitution of the nation Israel in 1948. Following the idea that a biblical generation was about 40 years, these people argued that within about a generation of Israel once again becoming a nation, the return of Jesus would occur (that is, by 1988). However, Jesus never said that the fig tree represented Israel. Rather, He used the imagery of the fig tree as an illustration and not as a prophetic symbol. Besides, this 40-year theory cannot apply because we are well past 1988.

Other interpreters of the verse contend that "this generation" refers to those who were living during Jesus' days and that the prophecies of Matthew 24–25 were fulfilled in some way in AD 70 through the Roman invasion of Jerusalem. Yet a careful look at the "all these things" (the preceding events of Matthew 24:4-33) clearly reveals they did not occur in the first-century destruction of Jerusalem. Thus Jesus had to be pointing to a different generation and time period—one that is yet future.

In the Olivet Discourse, Jesus is giving an extended prophetic discussion about events that have yet to occur even in our own day. The phrases "this generation" and "these things" are linked together by context and grammar in such a way that Jesus must be speaking of a future generation. Jesus is stating that a future generation will experience the events described in Matthew 24:4-33—"these things." These future people will not die until all the events are literally fulfilled.

When will this occur? It happens during the seven-year Tribulation (Daniel 9:24-27), which follows the rapture of the church as predicted in 1 Thessalonians 4:15-18. The Tribulation will be the most traumatic and terrible time in human history, and it is the members of this Tribulation generation to whom Jesus is speaking. "This generation" does not refer to people who lived in the first century or to our current generation. Rather, it is a yet future generation (though it could be very near and include people now living). The generation that sees the Tribulation is the same generation that will see the second coming of Jesus. From a prophetic perspective, *this generation* will therefore be the greatest generation.

TJD

MARK 7:15

There is nothing outside the man which
can defile him if it goes into him; but
the things which proceed out of the
man are what defile the man.

What can defile people?

If people choose to frequent lounges where alcohol is sold, visit the corner adult bookstore, hang around vulgar people, or view questionable movies at the local cinema, they certainly would be negatively influenced by such choices, but do these activities defile or corrupt them? Absolutely not! Misdeeds, inappropriate behaviors, or distasteful materials are snapshots of the heart, that is, they are the product of corruption, not its producer. Each person's heart is "more deceitful than all else and is desperately sick" (Jeremiah 17:9; see Matthew 15:18; 23:25-26; Titus 1:15-16). So which statement is true: "If you read that material, it will defile you," or "You read that kind of material because you are defiled"?

Warning people about the dangers of alcohol abuse, sexual indiscretion, or overindulgence is necessary, especially for the protection of innocent and vulnerable children and immature people. However, the reason they are dangerous to people is not because they are the cause of defilement, but because people are by nature defiled—we fancy the wrong fruit. The deeper issue is with who and what we are. We, like many before us, tend to focus more on outside influences than we do on maturing or strengthening our own internal weaknesses. Without our selfish and deceitful hearts, none of the evils we fear would even exist.

A virus is not the real threat to a computer; rather, it is a deficiency within the computer that makes it vulnerable. Also, lightning is not a threat to a television; it is the television's inability to defend itself. The computer and the television are their own worst enemies, as are we. Add a firewall to the computer or a surge protector to the TV, and the same external threats lose their power and influence.

The bad behaviors of the world are only as influential as the condition of the heart they confront. "The good man out of the good treasure of his heart brings forth what is good; and the evil man out of the evil treasure brings forth what is evil; for his mouth speaks from that which fills his heart" (Luke 6:45). So the question becomes, what makes a good man good? Or what "surge protector" or "firewall" can help a person overcome his own defilement and its effects? We must connect our hearts and minds to the antithesis of evil itself: God, in the person of Jesus, who leads us to the Father through the sanctifying work of the Holy Spirit.

Our own spiritual bankruptcy creates the evils that come from and against us. God reinvests in us through the blood of His Son and ensures our destiny "through faith for a salvation ready to be revealed in the last time" (1 Peter 1:3-5; Acts 4:12; Titus 3:4-7; Hebrews 12:1-3). God is everything incorruptible; without Him, we know only corruption. Incorporate God into every aspect of your life, and you will more clearly understand the threats of this world and handle them with grace.

GPS

49

WORDS NOT SPOKEN LIGHTLY

~ ❋ ~

MARK 8:33

He rebuked Peter, and said,
"Get behind Me, Satan;
for you are not setting your mind
on God's interests, but man's."

Was Jesus saying that Peter was possessed by the devil?

Peter was the most outspoken of Jesus' disciples. He appears to have been the boldest, the most outwardly enthusiastic, and the most abrasive of Jesus' inner circle of followers. He could say the right things at the right time, but often, he said the wrong things at the wrong time. One example of this is Mark 8:27-33.

In this passage, also recorded in Matthew 16:13-23, Peter correctly answers Jesus' question about His true identity, telling Jesus, "You are the Christ" (Mark 8:29). This short declaration is certainly one of the most perceptive and profound statements that anyone could speak. Jesus is indeed the Messiah. But when Jesus begins to teach the disciples about His upcoming death and resurrection—matters that were very important for the disciples to understand—Peter begins to rebuke Jesus, and Jesus counters Peter sharply, rebuking him and calling him Satan.

Jesus was being very straightforward, teaching the disciples about His role as the Messiah and the suffering He would endure as the fulfillment of Old Testament prophecies. The crucifixion was the whole purpose of His coming to earth from heaven and taking on human form even though He was the second person of the Trinity. Never before with the disciples had Jesus spoken so clearly and decisively about His divine mission, and Peter's strong reaction shows that the disciples understood Jesus' words.

Peter's impetuous action received a sharp rebuke from Jesus. In the same way that Jesus vocally silenced demons, He now abruptly stopped and silenced Peter (Mark 1:25). Peter's inability or unwillingness to accept Jesus as a suffering Savior was a rebellious refusal to accept the plan and will of God. God's plans and purposes are beyond our understanding (Isaiah 55:8-11).

Jesus' pronouncement of Peter as Satan was not a personal attack on Peter, but rather a use of hyperbole, rhetoric, and exaggeration to make a point for all the disciples and to get their attention. Jesus was telling them that Peter was being just like Satan, who tried to divert Jesus from fulfilling God's plan by tempting Jesus when He was in the desert (Matthew 4:1-11; Mark 1:12-13; Luke 4:1-13). Peter's thoughts and words, perhaps even initiated by Satan or spoken by Satan through Peter, were contradictory to God's plan. No words or person were going to divert Jesus' attention from fulfilling His mission on earth. Perhaps Peter, like many of his day, was thinking that Jesus was a Messiah who would lead the Jews out from under political oppression. If so, then crucifixion and death would prevent this freedom. Regardless of the nature or intent of Peter's thoughts, his words were wrong.

Jesus was not saying Peter was demon possessed. Demons or Satan cannot possess Christians, who are indwelt continuously by the Holy Spirit from the moment of conversion (1 Corinthians 3:16; 6:19; Colossians 1:13). Satan can afflict and tempt Christians, but he cannot possess or reside in them (Ephesians 2:1-3; 1 Thessalonians 2:18). The oppression for Christians is always external rather than internal.

In a world filled with words—in print, in the media, in conversations, in classrooms, in the workplace, and even in our thoughts—we should never take lightly Jesus' words and teaching. They are truth, and they tell us of eternal life and the free offer of it to all who believe, as Peter proclaimed, that Jesus is indeed the Messiah.

TJD

50

THE ULTIMATE LOSS

~ ❀ ~

MARK 8:35

Whoever wishes to save his life will
lose it, but whoever loses his life for My
sake and the gospel's will save it.

What does Jesus mean when He talks about
people losing or saving their lives?

Nothing in this passage refers to saving oneself from physical death, although a proper relationship with God does limit the number of ways death can claim its victims. The saving of life and the losing of life refer to choices in this life that affect one's *eternal* destiny.

How does a person save his life eternally? Or how is the whole of one's life preserved? Three separate comments by the Lord answer this question. 1) Jesus had gathered His disciples together to inform them about His coming death, burial, and resurrection. The apostle Peter finds this revelation unacceptable and rebukes Jesus for suggesting such a fate (Mark 8:31-32). 2) Jesus responds to Peter's rebuke by telling him and the other disciples that they should devote their minds to the matters that are of interest to God and refrain from imposing their own preferences onto His agenda. After all, a follower of Christ denies his own leanings (denies himself) and takes up the mantle or shield (cross) of God (8:33-34). 3) Following the verse in question, Jesus immediately looks at the end result of the choice we all must make: the forfeiture or saving of the soul. Do we pursue the interests of natural humanity or the interests of God? The former might and sometimes does produce tremendous advantages in the present life, but it will not satisfy the eternal or entire need of the soul (8:36-37).

In order for people's lives to be saved, they must gladly forfeit their own understandings or interests in favor of God's, through which the issues of life both now and into eternity are resolved in the death, burial, and resurrection of His beloved Son. All who genuinely desire to acquire the best in life must understand death as merely another kind of transition in life, which is eternal rather than temporal. A person who sees life through God's lens understands life, its blessings and curses, and most importantly, the remedy for its shortcomings: salvation in Christ. Too many fail or refuse to see God's benevolent role in His pursuit of humankind, and therefore they spend their lives trying to make their mark on the world before life passes them by. In truth, we ultimately forfeit everything if we live to make *our mark* on the world; it is better for all if we struggle to make *His mark* on the world. Only by accepting God's exclusive remedy for man's waywardness can we resolve the issues of life and soul. Just as Jesus warned the disciples not to do the work of Satan by denying the truth of His role as Son of God and Savior of man (8:31-33), so we too must ensure that our flawed or shortsighted interests don't interfere with the message of God's soul-saving grace. The cross—Christ's death and subsequent resurrection—is what the world needs. *His* marks save souls, not ours.

Each person is responsible to lose his or her life (dreams, interests, and understandings) to be eternally saved (through accepting and appreciating God's perspective). In the fog that clouds our minds, we must unashamedly trust in God who lights the way (8:38).

GPS

51

A SIGHT TO REMEMBER

~ ❈ ~

MARK 9:1

Jesus was saying to them,
"Truly I say to you, there are some of
those who are standing here who will not
taste death until they see the kingdom of
God after it has come with power."

When did anyone see the kingdom of God before dying?

Almost everyone has had an experience so memorable, either for better or worse, that afterward they said something like "You should have seen it," or "I will never forget it," or "I couldn't believe my eyes." Such an experience is exactly what Jesus was speaking of when He declared in Mark 9:1 that some people would see the kingdom of God before they died. And it did not take long for the words to come to fruition. Within a week, three of Jesus' disciples had that very experience.

The "some" of whom Jesus spoke are Peter, James, and John, Jesus' closest disciples, His inner circle. These were the only disciples Jesus took with Him into Jairus' home when He raised Jairus' daughter from the dead (Matthew 9:18-26), and they would be the only ones who went with Jesus into the heart of Gethsemane on the night of His arrest (Mark 14:33). For the experience of the present verse, Jesus took this trio of friends up to the top of a mountain, very possibly Mount Hermon, the highest in the land at 9200 feet above sea level. Here, on what has come to be known as the Mount of Transfiguration, they would briefly see Jesus in

113

a glorified body, full of divine splendor and majesty. Jesus is transformed into a brilliant and glorious figure shining like lightning.

Just as Moses had experienced a similar event on Mount Sinai (Exodus 34:29-34), now these three receive a momentary look at things to come. It is a sneak preview of what God has in plan for Jesus and the future, a confirmation from heaven that everything Jesus has spoken and taught during His earthly ministry is true (Mark 9:7).

Until this point, much of Jesus' divine nature had been concealed. But now these three friends and followers catch a glimpse of Jesus in full glory. And it was a sight to remember, one they would never forget. Years later, Peter would recount this experience, using it as a confirmation of the truth of the gospel, reminding his readers, "We did not follow cleverly devised tales when we made known to you the power and coming of our Lord Jesus Christ, but we were eyewitnesses of His majesty" (2 Peter 1:16).

The disciples saw a glimpse of the glorious future that awaits all those who believe in Jesus Christ. What they saw, they never forgot.

TJD

52

ONLY ONE

~ ❄ ~

MARK 10:18

And Jesus said to him, "Why do you call
Me good? No one is good except God."

**Was Jesus actually saying that He
Himself was not good?**

These words are Jesus' response to a man who asked Him, "Good Teacher, what shall I do to inherit eternal life?" (Mark 10:17). Verse 18 appears like a passing shot, which Jesus does not explain before moving quickly to answer his question. The man apparently caught Jesus' meaning because his subsequent address to Jesus leaves out the word *good* (10:20). This adjective and Jesus' response to it have eternal ramifications. For in Christ, who is indeed God, divine goodness or righteousness is imputed or credited to each person who is willing to admit his or her inability to do what is required to inherit eternal life. The rich young man is incapable of being good enough to save his own soul, as are we.

A person is only good in Christ. As creatures made in the image of God, we are able to do good things, but we are not good by nature. We are lawbreakers. "For whoever keeps the whole law and yet stumbles in one point, he has become guilty of all" (James 2:10-11). Centuries of recorded human history and an honest evaluation of one's own personal attitudes and actions combine to confirm Scripture's assessment of humanity's selfish, unrighteous leanings. The apostle Paul, echoing Psalm 14:1-3, depicts humanity's real state of mind: "There is none righteous, not even one; there is none who understands, there is none who seeks for God;

All have turned aside, together they have become useless; there is none who does good, there is not even one" (Romans 3:10-12).

The fact is that God alone is good, just as Jesus claims, and from Him emanates every sort of goodness known to angels and man. Consider God's initial response to Moses' desire for God to show him His glory. The characteristic that Moses will see only partially, but that demonstrates God's glory preeminently, is His goodness (Exodus 33:18-19). Only in relationship to God can goodness be attributed to us. Apart from Him, we are but self-appointed moral arbiters living in a perpetual state of spiritual death, unable to be perfectly good because we are unable to see God perfectly (Isaiah 64:5-7).

Neither the rich young man nor any of us have the quality within ourselves to do what God requires to receive eternal life, which is to obey every statute in the Law. Therefore, we who lack Christ's goodness—His perfection—must somehow obtain it. This is done through individual faith in Christ's substitutionary death—His willingness to accept upon Himself the guilt of others and to die in their place. By accepting His death as ours, we acquire His state of goodness and remove ourselves from the condemnation of the Law (Romans 5:17-19; 8:1). The reward of such faith is eternal life.

If we must boast, let us boast in the goodness that we have in Christ, for He alone is the Good Teacher. We are His apprentices. Our goodness is not of our own making; it's our Mentor's gift to us (Jeremiah 9:24; 1 Corinthians 1:30-31).

GPS

53

CAUTION! DANGEROUS TO YOUR HEALTH

~ ☀ ~

MARK 16:18

*They will pick up serpents, and if
they drink any deadly poison,
it will not hurt them; they will lay hands
on the sick, and they will recover.*

**Are Christians really guaranteed the ability to
handle snakes and drink poison without harm?**

Confusion about this verse is not so much theological as it is textual. The statement is very clear but the greater question is whether this verse is indeed part of the Bible. It is part of one of the most difficult and disputed textual problems in the New Testament. Did Jesus really speak these words, and did the Holy Spirit really preserve them by inspiring Mark to include them in his record? Were this verse and those around it part of Mark's original writing or not?

The last 12 verses of Mark (16:9-20), known as "the longer ending," are not found in the oldest and most reliable manuscripts of Mark's Gospel, and the style and wording in the verses also lead many interpreters to the conclusion that the verses are not part of the book and should not be viewed as authentic. The verses are in the majority of Greek manuscripts, but this occurs because of multiple copies of these manuscripts being made. The awkward transition between verses 8 and 9 also strengthens the case for the verses being added by an unknown source sometime after Mark finished his writing.

Additionally, more than one variation of the 12 verses exist in the manuscript history of the passage. Many of the early church fathers, including Clement, Origen, and Eusebius, had access to the entire Bible, but they seem to be unaware of these verses. Most of the content of the verses is found elsewhere in the Bible, and therefore, if the verses are omitted, no truth is lost. The proper truths are not in question, but the proper text is.

Although the declarations of verse 18 are not explicitly stated in other passages, there are biblical examples of much, though not all, of the verse. Acts 28:3-6 records an instance of involuntary snake handling without harm, but the Bible does not record anyone drinking poison. Using this passage as proof of God's protection if one engaged in such acts would be unwise.

The issue in Mark 16:9-20 is not that readers are missing part of the Bible, and therefore we have less than 100 percent of the Bible. Rather, because of the history of the copying and transmission of the original manuscripts of the Bible (none of which have survived), we have in effect more than 100 percent of the Bible. The task of serious students of God's Word is to determine the true words of Scripture. Some verses simply should not be considered authentic (however, none of the verses in question pertain to major doctrines of the Bible). The last 12 verses of Mark are some of the few verses in this category. They were in circulation by the middle of the second century, about a hundred years after Mark wrote, but they are not likely his words.

TJD

54

YOU'VE GOT TO BE KIDDING!

LUKE 6:28

Bless those who curse you, pray for those who mistreat you.

Should we permit abuse?

The way in which the individual Christian responds to maltreatment depends on the way one understands the difference between personal and social ethics and behavior. The Sermon on the Mount reflects the Lord's attitudes about Christians' personal or individual behavior in relationship to others, especially unbelievers. It does not lay out the actions and attitudes of the state—or the people who are acting on its behalf—which has the responsibility of judgment and punishment (Romans 13:1-6).

God causes "His sun to rise on the evil and the good, and sends rain on the righteous and the unrighteous" (Matthew 5:45). If God lets His blessing fall on everyone, then each individual representative of God should do the same. "To live as Christ" is the mantra of the believer. A Christian's life is not about "me and my interests," it's about God and His interests. "Love your enemies, and do good, and lend, expecting nothing in return; and your reward will be great, and you will be sons of the Most High; for He Himself is kind to ungrateful and evil men. Be merciful, just as your Father is merciful" (Luke 6:35-36). The Sermon on the Mount teaches us not to treat people the way we are treated, but to treat them the way we would have them treat us (Luke 6:31). It is natural to want to retaliate against someone who belittles your mother or injures your little brother, but it is supernatural to leave the judgment and punishment to the state and respond to the perpetrator the way you would hope victims of your folly would respond to you. To love the lovely and give to those who can pay you back are easy acts, but to love the unlovely and give without any expectation of receiving something in return are divine (Luke 6:32-34).

The kingdom of heaven on earth is at odds with the social norm. Its presence is an unwanted but necessary gift to the world that often generates contempt. Still, it is the grace of God given to a godless world for its own good, and we are its ambassadors chosen from the world for it (2 Corinthians 5:17-20). And since God offered the gospel without partiality to both Gentile and Jew, rich and poor (Acts 10:34), and in Christ showed the world divine humility for the benefit of all (Philippians 2:5-9), who are we that we should do less? Those who are forgiven have received unmerited grace, and Christ has received them into the family of God. They cannot in good conscience deny such blessings to others (Ephesians 4:32).

The Sermon on the Mount does not prevent you from restraining those who may try to irreparably harm you or another. Turning the other cheek (Mark 6:29) reflects a selfless attitude that expresses vulnerability and resists retaliation. It is not a recipe for getting pulverized. Jesus' statements require that we patiently and proactively seek to do what is right for those who speak evil of us and to pray for our abusers, even in spite of them (Romans 12:14-18). We are to love our enemies, that is, love those we hate (Psalm 5:4-6) with selfless and benevolent acts. In so doing, we accurately represent the character of our heavenly Father.

GPS

55

FIRST THINGS FIRST

~ ✽ ~

LUKE 9:60

Allow the dead to bury their own dead.

What does Jesus mean by this instruction?

Being a Christian, a disciple of Jesus Christ, is not a matter to be taken lightly. The cost of commitment is very high, and Jesus repeatedly told His followers that discipleship must be a priority in each of their lives (Matthew 4:19-20; 16:24; 19:21). Discipleship takes precedence over all other social, cultural, and familial obligations. It requires a radical commitment to Jesus Christ. Luke 9:57-62 emphasizes this fact three times with encounters between Jesus and three prospective disciples. In this context, Jesus makes the very pointed comment about death and burial.

The proper burial of family members was (and remains) a very significant event in Judaism. Burial of the dead was a religious obligation of extreme urgency and importance, taking priority even over the study of the Law (Genesis 50:5; Leviticus 21:1-3). Failure to provide a proper burial was scandalous. Luke 9:59 does not clearly state whether the would-be disciple's father is already dead or is about to die. If the father had already died, the son would have already been involved in the funeral process. Therefore, the son was probably waiting for the death of his father, after which he would provide a funeral and possibly also gain an inheritance. He is asking for more time before following Jesus as a disciple.

Jesus' enigmatic response about burying the dead is a pun in which Jesus is saying let the spiritually dead bury the physically dead. The Bible teaches that non-Christians are spiritually dead (John 5:25; Romans

6:13; Ephesians 2:1; 5:14). Jesus sees that the young man making the request has been spiritually awakened and understands that Jesus is the Messiah. He is now telling the man that the proclamation of the gospel must be his new priority. The desire to properly bury a family member was one of the best excuses for postponing discipleship, but it wasn't satisfactory. Other family members or people who are not believers can take care of the funeral. Instead of permitting the individual to fulfill religious, cultural, and familial expectations, Jesus is giving him a new and greater priority.

The Christian author and apologist C.S. Lewis wrote, "All that is not eternal is eternally out of date." Jesus is communicating this same sense of priority and urgency to a prospective follower in this encounter in Luke 9:59-60. When a person becomes a Christian, everything else must be realigned. Commitment to Jesus Christ takes priority over everything else in life including friends, work, cultural expectations, and even family. Each of these is important, but not as important as following Jesus Christ. When a decision must be made between God and something else—whatever it may be—God must come first.

TJD

LUKE 11:29

As the crowds were increasing, He began to
say, "This generation is a wicked generation;
it seeks for a sign, and yet no sign will
be given to it but the sign of Jonah."

What is the sign of Jonah?

This phrase is used in Matthew 12:39 and 16:4, although in 16:4, Jesus doesn't elaborate on the phrase—He simply walks away from the crowd. These passages and others (Mark 8:11; John 2:18; 4:48; see 1 Corinthians 1:22) show that the people to whom Jesus ministered were seldom willing to take Him at His word. Their disbelief was so deep that even miracles, which they had either seen or heard about, required some secondary sign as evidence that He was whom He claimed (Matthew 12:22; Luke 16:14-16). No wonder He viewed the generation of His time as evil, wicked, and adulterous. But we should not be too quick to judge them as inferior to our own or more perverse. "Prove it!" or "Give me some extra-biblical evidence to support what the Bible says," people say to those who witness on behalf of the Lord. The problem both then and now is therefore not one of credible evidence, but one of incredible unbelief. No sign would have been good enough, and Jesus was not about to give them one—except the sign of Jonah.

Interpreters who consider Matthew 12:40 a late typological addition to the text understand the sign as "the preaching of repentance." However, if 12:40 is authentic ("Just as Jonah was three days and three nights in the belly of the sea monster, so will the Son of Man be three days and three nights in the heart of the earth"), it corresponds to Luke's less specific comment in 11:30 ("For just as Jonah became a sign to the Ninevites, so will the Son of Man be to this generation"). Note that the sign in Matthew 12:39 and Luke 11:29 is future to Jesus' statement. He is not referring to His past preaching, that is, a sign given by Him, but of something yet to take place. Jonah personally overcame judgment or calamity through obedience, and through obedience Jesus, on behalf of all humankind, would overcome judgment to live again. Jonah's deliverance points to an even greater deliverance not yet realized. His personal deliverance foreshadows a deliverance that would be universal.

Through Jonah, Jesus is pointing to Himself. "Just as Jonah became a sign to the Ninevites, so will the Son of Man be to this generation (Luke 11:30). In Christ alone is deliverance possible! To the unbelieving sign-seeking Pharisees and scribes, and to their followers, Jesus is saying He is the only sign they are going to get (see John 2:18-19). But unlike the Ninevites and the Queen of Sheba, who believed Jonah and Solomon, the generation of Jesus' day would question the Messenger of messengers to their own demise (Matthew 12:41-42; Luke 11:31-32). To all generations, Jesus says: "Blessed are those who hear the word of God and observe it" (Luke 11:28). Though the message is not the sign, it most certainly identifies it—Him!

GPS

57
THE GREAT DIVIDE
~ ✳ ~

LUKE 12:51

*Do you suppose that I came to grant peace
on earth? I tell you, no, but rather division.*

Didn't Jesus come to bring peace?

We often hear people ask, "Can't we all just get along?" Competing ideas in a multicultural world will naturally bring various degrees of conflict ranging from honest debate to wanton destruction. Without a single standard by which people govern themselves, people vie for power and influence while others flock to those leaders whose beliefs suit their own self-interests. Modern debate revolves around the issue of who determines what is true or best: humankind (with its secular and religious philosophies) or the Lord God.

The world into which Jesus was born generally found truth among the gods and their representatives. Truth seemed incomprehensible to many, including Pontius Pilate: "What is truth?" (John 18:38). But for the most part, truth was an absolute for which philosophers and theologians alike devoted their lives. As research into the physical world advanced, scientists joined the humanists in search of the illusive parts that make up the whole of truth. Then, in the late twentieth century and now in the twenty-first century, truth became culture-based and standardless (which ultimately means godless). This makes tolerance humanity's only absolute virtue in an attempt to avoid the inevitable consequences that come with an ever-shrinking world: divisiveness and conflict.

Nonetheless, truth demands but one source, and for it to be absolute, that source must be divine. Also, the people must have a nature that understands its best interests are found in a proper relationship with the divine mind. Herein lies the problem. Since the early days of creation, humankind has taken its freedom to choose in the wrong direction (Genesis 3:1-7; Galatians 5:13-15). Rather than pursue God, it has pursued its own self-interests, which are as numerable as the stars in the heavens. From that time to this, a gracious and compassionate God, who actually dislikes judgment, has become the pursuer (Exodus 34:6-7; Jonah 4:2; 2 Peter 3:9). However, society is so deceived and defiant that each time He injects truth into it, the reaction is similar to that of putting salt into an open wound. God the Father knew that the injection of His Son into the affairs of humankind would produce such a reaction—one that would result in the killing of His Son (Luke 12:49-50). Either He creates the reaction with His presence or He chooses to leave us without a Savior. Real truth penetrating pretentious truth always produces storm clouds, but in the storm clouds is the rain that brings life.

The peace and unity for which so many long will come only at the foot of the cross of Christ (1 Corinthians 1:18-25). In this life, the testimony of truth and the peace it affords can be found only in the church, if we are willing to submit to the God of Scripture and His Son. "Now I exhort you, brethren, by the name of our Lord Jesus Christ, that you all agree and that there be no divisions among you, but you be made complete in the same mind and in the same judgment"(1 Corinthians 1:10). Christ's purpose in coming to this earth will only bring unity to those who identify with Him; all others will find Him and those who trust in Him offensive beyond measure (Luke 12:52-53; John 15:18-21).

GPS

JOHN 7:38

He who believes in Me, as the Scripture said,
"'From his innermost being will
flow rivers of living water."

What Bible passage is Jesus referring to here? Did Jesus misquote the Bible?

Almost 10 percent of the New Testament is comprised of citations of or allusions to the Old Testament. Jesus frequently cited the Old Testament during His life and ministry, and His use of it is recorded throughout the four Gospels.

If a citation in the New Testament does not match word-for-word with the Old Testament counterpart, the New Testament speaker did not make an error. Rather, he is using the earlier passage in a nuanced and technical way that requires careful attention. That is precisely what is occurring when Jesus speaks in John 7:38.

While observing the annual seven-day Feast of Tabernacles (Leviticus 23:33-36) commemorating God's provision for the Israelites in bringing them out of slavery in Egypt, Jesus alluded to an Old Testament passage that He fulfilled. Every day during the celebration, priests drew water from the Pool of Siloam to carry and pour on the altar at the temple. While doing this they recited Isaiah 12:3: "You will joyously draw water from the springs of salvation." This ritual commemorated God's provision of water for the thirsty Israelites during their wilderness sojourn and anticipated a yet future time of blessing for them.

When on the last day of the feast Jesus said that those who believe in Him would experience "rivers of living water" flowing from within them, He was speaking of the ministry of the Holy Spirit (John 7:39) and using an annual religious ritual as a picture of a perpetual spiritual peace and blessing. When Jesus said, "as the Scripture said" (7:38), He did not identify the specific Old Testament passage or passages He had in mind, and no single verse matches His words exactly. Among the most likely verses from which He was drawing are Psalm 78:15-16; Isaiah 44:3; 58:11; and Zechariah 14:8. Although we cannot dogmatically determine the specific verse, Jesus' words reflect the common biblical symbolism of water and spiritual blessing. Those who heard Him would have immediately understood Him.

The writers of the New Testament quoted the Old Testament between 250 and 300 times, and the citations occur in almost every book of the New Testament. Sometimes these were cited word-for-word, but on other occasions the references were paraphrased or summarized. On occasion New Testament writers combined verses from separate Old Testament passages, and at other times they changed the grammar or omitted certain portions.

Allusions are even more frequent, and lists of them vary from 400 to 4000. These include references to events, people, or phrases from the Old Testament. New Testament writers drew from the Old Testament for many reasons. Sometimes they acknowledged the fulfillment of an Old Testament prediction or prophecy (see Isaiah 7:14 and Matthew 1:22-23). Other times they drew parallels between New Testament and Old Testament incidents. On other occasions, a New Testament person uses verses for emphasis to relate Old Testament terminology or concepts to the audience. How a verse is used must be carefully examined in every instance.

The study of the use of the Old Testament in the New Testament is a rich and rewarding endeavor. Like a complex puzzle or unfolding mystery, it brings unique challenges. Yet the use of the Old Testament in the New Testament is also an evidence of the ministry of the Holy Spirit in inspiring the words of the Bible and guiding its writers. The flow and continuity of the plan of God throughout the ages and between the two testaments is reaffirmed every time the Old Testament is cited in the New Testament.

TJD

YOU CAN'T SAY THAT!

~ ❋ ~

JOHN 10:34

Has it not been written in your Law,
"I SAID, YOU ARE GODS"?

Did Jesus teach that human beings are gods?

Jesus frequently quoted the Old Testament in His teaching and preaching. By so doing He showed the progression, continuity, and prophetic fulfillment of God's revelation in inspired Scripture. In John 10:34, Jesus uses the Old Testament to bolster an argument and defense when His life is threatened by an angry crowd. He does this by using a passage from Psalms and calling it "your Law."

The word *Law* usually refers to the first five books of the Bible, but in Jesus' time it often referred to all of the Old Testament. In the context of Psalm 82:1,6, "gods" did not describe deities but rather authorities, specifically the leaders of Israel. The psalmist Asaph was declaring that unjust judges, even though they were given the title *gods* because of their function and because they declared life-and-death judgments, would die like all people. They had exalted positions and responsibilities but human bodies. They were declared gods, yet they died.

Jesus then builds on this Old Testament passage when the Jews wanted to stone Him for blasphemy after He declared "I and the Father are one" (John 10:30). What was not literally true of the judges of Psalm 82 (that they would be gods) was a reality for Jesus. He was God. Old Testament judges could be called "gods" because they were instruments of the Word of God. How much more so then did Jesus deserve to be called God, since He is truly God and the Word of God incarnate (John 1:14). What they were in name, He is by nature. Jesus is using a common form of rabbinic argument of His day, arguing from the lesser to the greater.

Careless rather than careful reading and interpretation of the Bible quickly leads to misunderstanding, confusion, and doctrinal error. This is certainly true of John 10:34, a passage that if taken out of context seems to teach that people are divine. Such a blurring of the Creator and creature distinction is common in pagan and non-Christian thought. Whether one speaks of a divine spark within, an inner light, or a progression from humanity to deity, such teachings are all unbiblical. All human beings are created in the image and likeness of God and therefore have intrinsic dignity and worth, but we are not divine. Christians will one day have glorified bodies like Jesus' post-resurrection body (1 John 3:2), but the Bible never teaches that Christians are or will be gods.

TJD

60

THE GOOD DEATH

~ ✻ ~

JOHN 12:32

And I, if I am lifted up from the earth,
will draw all men to Myself.

Will everyone be saved?

There are two phrases of interest in this passage. "If I am lifted up from the earth" refers to the manner in which Christ will die (lifted up on a cross), as the next verse shows. The crowd also accepts this understanding. Knowing that the messianic reign will "remain forever" (John 12:34), it is perplexed by the prediction of His impending death. The second phrase, "I will draw all men to myself," is sometimes incorrectly understood to mean that God in His boundless grace will, through Christ's death, save everyone past and present (this is known as *universalism* or *inclusivism*). However, this interpretation is not consistent with the biblical record.

The word "draw" means "to tug, attract, or lure." In this context, Jesus lures "all men" to Himself through His death, resurrection, and ascension. However, the biblical record is clear: all men will not be saved. "The sea gave up the dead which were in it, and death and Hades gave up the dead which were in them; and they were judged, every one of them, according to their deeds. Then death and Hades were thrown into the lake of fire. This is the second death, the lake of fire" (Revelation 20:13-14; see also Matthew 25:41; 2 Peter 3:1-7,10-13). To suggest that God will forcibly draw all people into His kingdom and that none will experience eternal condemnation, even if they openly and willfully despise and reject God and His Son, is to go against the clear teaching of Scripture. Though the

Lord certainly desires all to be saved (2 Peter 3:9), many will reject Him irreversibly (Matthew 18:6-7). People can be drawn or lured by many things (Deuteronomy 30:17-18), but the idea does not suggest that the one being lured will or must take the bait.

"Draw all men" therefore does not refer to universal salvation, but rather to the indiscriminate dissemination of the gospel of Christ to every nation and people. Jesus is well aware that His words are in response to the concerns of a Greek audience (John 12:20). He wants to assure them that salvation, though of the Jews, is not the sole property of the Jews, but is offered to "all men" without impartiality (Acts 19:8-10; 20:21; Romans 1:16; 2:9-11; 10:11-13).

As the bronze serpent was "lifted up" on a pole to provide victory over imminent death (Numbers 21:5-9; John 3:14-15), so Christ would be "lifted up" on the cross to bring victory to anyone who looks to Him for victory over death (see John 12:23-24,27). If God does not draw or lure people to the light, all remain in darkness (John 6:44,65). By dying and making the gospel of His saving grace available to anyone who would accept it, Jesus provides a channel through which individuals from every nation can pass to successfully negate the widespread influence of the ruler of this age: Satan and his demonic cronies (John 12:31). The cross ensures the defeat of Satan. Through His death on the cross, His resurrection from the dead, and His ascension into heaven, Jesus creates a door and entices us to knock. Knock, and He will open it and give you entrance into His eternal kingdom.

GPS

61

FIRE FROM HEAVEN

~ ❋ ~

ACTS 2:3,11

There appeared to them tongues as
of fire distributing themselves, and
they rested on each one of them.

What actually happened on the Day of Pentecost?

When an individual speaks to the United Nations, each person listening hears the speech simultaneously in his own language through a headset linked to a translator. Though a helpful picture of what took place on the Day of Pentecost in first-century Jerusalem, this modern miracle of technology pales in comparison to the ancient miracle of God. The disciples became instant testimonials of the powerful presence of God through the baptism of the Holy Spirit (see Acts 1:4-8; 11:15-16). Miraculously, every person heard the disciples praising God in his or her own language.

The presence of wind with fire is telling. Both the Hebrew and Greek words used to identify the Spirit of God refer to either wind, to breath, or to spirit. The idea of the Spirit of God coming upon a people to rejuvenate them spiritually (breathing life into them) is not alien to Jewish thinking. The restoration of Israel by the Holy Spirit was a constant hope (Ezekiel 37:9-14). Fire is connected with the presence of God (Exodus 13:21-22; 19:18; 40:34-38; Deuteronomy 4:36), the Angel of the Lord (Exodus 3:2-6), and (by John the Baptist) the Holy Spirit (Matthew 3:11). Wind and fire describe the power and presence of God, here specifically in the person of the Holy Spirit (Acts 2:4).

The phrase "tongues as of fire distributing themselves" is a description of the event by Luke, who, as a probable eyewitness (see Luke 1:1-2), describes the event from hindsight. The witnesses most likely did not see literal tongues flying around them, only the fiery-like visual moving around and then on them. The immediate ability of the apostles to speak in various dialects enables Luke to connect the reception of the gift of tongues (various dialects) back to the moment the Spirit of God came upon them.

The ability to speak foreign languages (known languages as opposed to ecstatic utterances—see Acts 2:4 and the use of the word "language" in verses 6,8) accompanied the baptism of the Spirit, which was the primary purpose for the sound and visual display. The ability to speak languages was the appropriate sign of God's presence for that specific moment in time. Jews from every nation (2:5,9-11) had returned to celebrate the second of three great pilgrimages to Jerusalem: the Feast of Weeks (or *Pentecost* in Greek), which refers to the celebration that took place 50 days after the Passover. Nothing else could have been more spectacular to this audience than seeing a group of provincial Galileans speaking fluently about the wonders of God in whatever language was needed (2:11). The majority knew that God was involved in this incident.

Every day a person comes to Christ, a baptism of the Spirit takes place, forever arming the believer with the power of God (Ephesians 1:13). How that power will be utilized depends on the faithfulness of the believer and the role God desires to give him or her. The ability to speak a language one does not know is but one of many gifts at God's disposal. Be faithful and be willing—God will use you as He deems fit.

GPS

62

COVERING THE BASES

~ ✳ ~

ACTS 17:23

*While I was passing through and
examining the objects of your worship,
I also found an altar with this inscription,
"TO AN UNKNOWN GOD."
Therefore what you worship in
ignorance, this I proclaim to you.*

**Why did the Athenians have an
altar to an unknown deity?**

Almost everyone knows what it means to "cover the bases" or "hedge the bets" in a circumstance. Rather than staking everything on one outcome, a person will spread the risk or reward over several options. This "just in case" or "just to make sure" attitude is common in financial strategies, gambling, and scores of other daily activities. But we wouldn't think people would do it in their religious lives. We want to think that surely people have more certainty and commitment on spiritual matters. Yet they don't, and that is exactly what the apostle Paul witnessed when he went to Athens and preached to the religious and intellectual leaders there during his second great missionary journey.

The Greeks, like the Babylonians before them, the Romans after them, and many other cultures practiced polytheism—the worship of many gods. Although idolatry is condemned in the Bible, it is still common. Practitioners of it in any form, ancient or contemporary, may be sincere, but they are wrong.

In their ignorance and spiritual blindness, the Athenians erected an altar to a nameless, faceless deity just to be sure they hadn't missed anything spiritually after erecting temples and altars to all the other gods in their pantheon. They practiced equal-opportunity idolatry.

The presence of such an altar and others is well attested in Greek history. More than a hundred years after Paul's first-century visit to Athens, the geographer Pausanias and philosopher Philostratus wrote about such altars in Athens. The specific altar Paul saw was probably erected about 600 years earlier during a plague in Athens. The Athenians built many altars and performed many sacrifices in attempts to halt its spread, but all to no avail. Then a man named Epimenides suggested that perhaps the Athenians had offended some unknown god, and so another altar was created, and eventually the plague ended. What Paul saw was likely this pagan memorial, and he used it as a reference point in his sermon to the Athenians.

Paul confronted the pagan belief system of the Athenians and proclaimed to them the true God of the Bible and salvation offered by Jesus Christ (Acts 17:24-34). He boldly articulated and defended his faith to the intellectuals, leaders, and skeptics of Athens. In so doing he provides an excellent model for engaging our own culture and society. Don't be fooled by false teaching, whether it is espoused from pulpits and podiums or on airwaves and bumper stickers. Know your culture, know your faith, and stand firm in the teachings of the Bible.

TJD

63

ONE GOD, ONE FAITH

~ ✸ ~

ROMANS 1:16

*I am not ashamed of the gospel, for it is the
power of God for salvation to everyone who
believes, to the Jew first and also to the Greek.*

Why are the Jews first?

To answer this question, we must ask two more: "To whom is Paul writing?" and "What does the phrase mean?"

Paul is clearly writing to the saints living in the city of Rome (Romans 1:7), but he is writing to a specific audience within that church. Note that he is talking to this group about the importance of ministering *to the Gentiles* (Romans 1:6,13-14). That group is Jewish believers, and the purpose of directing this letter to them is not to espouse the importance of justification by faith alone or faith without works, but rather to use this essential teaching on salvation to promote unity among believers, both Jew and Gentile (see Romans 2:9-13, where impartiality is the primary topic; 4:16; 10:12).

The first 11 chapters of Romans are clearly designed to show God's original intention to include Gentiles among the faithful (Romans 3:9,20,28-30; 4:16; 5:12-18; 9:22-24,30-33; 11:7-11). At the midpoint of chapter 11, Paul directly addresses the Gentiles to advise them that their inclusion among the faithful does not imply the end of Israel as a nation (Romans 11:13-36). A temporary hardening of the heart has occurred in Israel for a predetermined amount of time (through the time of the Gentiles, which extends from the Babylonian empire to the end of the Great Tribulation—11:25). In the same way that the disobedience of Israel brought the mercy of God to the Gentiles, so the eventual disobedience of the Gentiles will return God's mercy to the nation of Israel (Romans 11:28-32). The restoration of the Jews will begin in the Great Tribulation with the ministry of 144,000 Jews and culminate in the millennial kingdom. This hope would bring great encouragement to Paul's Roman audience, which had not forgotten God's promise to Abraham (Genesis 12:1-3).

Jesus discloses the meaning of the phrase "to the Jew first" during His discussion with the Samaritan woman (John 4:22). God's intention has always been to extend salvation to all peoples, but He chose to reach out to them through one people: the Jews. In a cordial discussion on comparable religions, Jesus addresses the Samaritan woman's understanding of multicultural relativism. He informs her that Samaritan worship is *not* the path through which God's salvation comes. Rather, it comes through the sacrificial system of the Jewish people, which culminates in His death, burial, and resurrection. True worship of God is achieved through the work of God's Holy Spirit and by the truth that is found only in the person of Jesus Christ (John 4:20-24). The phrases "salvation is from the Jews" and "to the Jew first" are not statements of superiority or priority of one people over another. Rather, they are merely statements of historical fact. God chose the nation of Israel to be the conduit of salvation for the people of every nation (see Romans 3:1-2).

Paul is primarily addressing the Jewish constituency in the Roman church for the sole purpose of promoting and defending the unifying goal of the gospel of Jesus Christ—all people of every kind in one faith serving the one true God. There is one God for every person and nation, and He is found through the faith that was revealed through Abraham and his seed and that culminates fully in the Son of David, the Lord Jesus Christ (Matthew 1:17).

GPS

64

FAITH FIRST

~ ✳ ~

ROMANS 3:31

Do we then nullify the Law through faith? May it
never be! On the contrary, we establish the Law.

> **By what means does salvation**
> **come to each individual?**

The answer to this question has been a cause of division among Christians from the first century to the present. Some have concluded that effort expended (works) to keep the Law of God will appease His wrath and keep His judgment in abeyance as long as that effort is sincere and continues. This naturally promotes a sense of accomplishment, since the effort to bring about one's salvation includes both the work of Christ *and* the work of the individual. Through this theological perspective, the Law of God is supposedly validated and appeased through the cross and human effort.

Others have argued that personal acceptance of (faith in) the sacrificial and substitutionary death, burial, and resurrection of Christ satisfies the unattainable requirements of the Law and results in the eternal security of the believer. Does the law of faith somehow then nullify or abolish the Law? Paul answers resoundingly, "No!" It establishes or validates the Law. The Law shows me my imperfections; it allows me to see the perfection of Christ. The Law convinces me that I cannot achieve perfection (be made righteous or justified) on my own; it convinces me to trust *not* in myself, but in Jesus through whom my righteousness is achieved. The Law is my instructor (Galatians 3:24-26), it encourages me to depend on and boast in God alone for righteousness (Romans 3:27; Ephesians 2:8-9), it keeps me ever mindful of my inability to do enough to save myself, and it tells me that I am sinful and will always fall short of acquiring righteousness on my own (Romans 3:10-20; 7:8-12; James 2:10).

The Just One compelled His Son, who knew no sin (2 Corinthians 5:21), to satisfy the many and righteous requirements of the Law by voluntarily shedding His blood on the cross as a covering for the unrighteousness of humanity so that He might become the "justifier" of those who by faith accept His death for sin as their own (Romans 3:26). Therefore the "Law through faith" does what the Law through works cannot—save the human soul from eternal death and separation from God. Faith in Christ's death establishes the Law; it satisfies the requirements of the Law and freely gives the gift of God's righteousness to anyone who trusts in Christ (Romans 3:22-24).

Good works, however, do play a prominent role in the Christian experience—they are the believer's response to the grace of God, which is received through faith (Ephesians 2:10; James 2:14-25). In appreciation for the salvation that God freely gives, the true believer naturally commits his or her life to the daily pursuit of holy or righteous living without fear of being cast out of the family of God for not doing quite enough. The believer's status in Christ is what does enough. No son loses his status as a son when his behavior falls short of an expected standard. Neither would God the Father disown one of His children (John 1:12; 10:27-30). Faith saves, justifies, or makes a soul righteous; good works reflect the person's awareness of this unmerited status and his or her desire to love God in return. Saving faith will always be accompanied by grateful works (Titus 1:16; 2:11-14; 3:1,8).

GPS

65

NOT AN EASY DELIVERY

~ ❋ ~

ROMANS 8:22

*We know that the whole creation groans
and suffers the pains of childbirth
together until now.*

How does the earth groan and suffer?

Sometimes women refer to a child's birth as an "easy" or "difficult" delivery. Such terms regarding the relative pains of childbirth are similar to the imagery Paul uses in his letter to the Romans.

When God created the world, it was good and without sin (Genesis 1:31). However, with the fall of Adam and Eve in the Garden of Eden, sin entered the world and affected every part of creation (Genesis 3:14-19; Romans 5:12). Humans were afflicted with a sin nature and the ramifications of it, and all of the world was subject to decay and destruction. This explains natural disasters as well as sickness and death among animals as well as humans.

In Romans 8:19-21, Paul discusses the interrelationship of people with the physical world. In these verses he tells his readers that God's plan for the ages includes a future restoration of creation that is related to the salvation of God's people. God previously judged the entire creation along with its inhabitants because of the sin of Adam and Eve. However, the curse will one day be reversed.

When God's program for salvation is finished, the creation itself will be freed from decay (Romans 8:21). This will begin with a re-creation and reordering at the second coming of Jesus Christ, continue into the thousand-year reign of Jesus Christ on the earth (Isaiah 11:5-9; 35:1-2,5-7), and end with the creation of a new heaven and a new earth in the eternal state (Revelation 21:1; 22:3). The millennial kingdom will bring about the harmony of all of creation, and all that was lost in the Garden of Eden will be restored. It will be a time of peace and prosperity, health and happiness, and great spiritual awareness. It will be all that people have longed for when through the centuries they prayed "Thy kingdom come."

Romans 8:22 provides the summation of Paul's teaching about the present creation. Just as pain and suffering are parts of childbirth, so too the world is in extended suffering and pain because of sin and is awaiting delivery from it in the future.

The emphasis of this passage is not purely ecological. Rather, Paul is teaching this truth about creation as an illustration and a reminder that the present suffering of Christians, like those of creation, are temporary (Romans 8:18,23,28). God has a plan for the world, but more importantly, God has a plan for the people of the world. For Christians, those who love Him, God uses everything that happens to them in that plan. That is a great comfort.

In a world filled with chaos, despair, corruption, violence, and rampant evil, the certainty of the millennium and the restoration of creation provide assurance that God has not abandoned His prophetic plan. We need not have anxiety or fear from the headlines. God is in control.

Nothing that happens to you is beyond God's knowledge or concern. God knows your trials and tribulations and understands your fears and tears. And even more significant, nothing in this world can separate you from God's love (Romans 8:37-39).

TJD

66

Not in the Genes

~ ❀ ~

ROMANS 9:6

They are not all Israel who are
descended from Israel.

How can a person not be of Israel
who is born of Jewish parents?

The answer to this question depends on what the term *Israel* means. The human race is a melting pot of nations stirred up in a cauldron of condemnation. Our only way out of the pot is the ladle of God's mercy. But is this mercy mostly limited to the children of one nation, Israel? The Jewish believers in the first-century church in Rome struggled with the Gentiles' inclusion in God's program of salvation. After all, salvation is of the Jews (Romans 2:17-20; 3:1-2; John 4:22). How had centuries of work with the Jewish people suddenly become focused on the Gentiles? Has the word of God failed because the term *Israel* was becoming more inclusive and broader than its bloodline (Romans 9:6)? Are the children of God known only by their ancestry? No! They are known by meeting God's conditions, by their compliance to His will and their faith in His promises (9:8). God's children are not identified by bloodline. They are defined by a common faith, and God alone decides the name by which they are called—Jew (Israel) or Christian.

God chose Abraham. Why not choose someone else from Ur or maybe from another city? What was so special about Ur? God decided that Sarah would give birth to a son and that through his bloodline Messiah would come. Why couldn't He have simply chosen Ishmael and saved

Sarah the trouble of going through a post-primetime pregnancy? Then God messes with the customary inheritance rights and chooses Jacob rather than his older brother Esau to be the father of Israel. Choosing Esau would have saved the family a lot of interpersonal friction (Romans 9:9-13). When human beings are unable to understand the reasons behind God's choices, perhaps the Lord should reconsider His options in the event He overlooked something that His beloved creatures noticed. Really! Could you picture an all-knowing and all-powerful God ruling the world by committee? What a waste of time!

Ishmael and Esau were Abraham's descendents, but they were not "of Israel." The line of promise stretched from Abraham through Isaac. Why? Because God decided it would! Since the crucifixion and resurrection of Jesus Christ, the responsibility for the spreading of the gospel has passed from the nation of Israel to the church—a compilation of peoples *from* all nations set apart by God *into* all nations. God decides who He will use and how He will use them to bring about salvation and eternal life. Into the pot of condemned humanity, God dips the ladle of His mercy to choose whom He will for whatever purpose He deems best for humanity (Romans 9:15-16,18,21-26). Being a child of God does not depend on ancestry; it depends on God's mercy!

The apostle Paul was not of "spiritual" Israel until he gave his life to Christ. "For he is not a Jew who is one outwardly; neither is circumcision that which is outward in the flesh. But he is a Jew who is one inwardly; and circumcision is that which is of the heart, by the Spirit; not by the letter; and his praise is not from men, but from God" (Romans 2:28-29). Jews who reject the gospel cannot be members of the family of God, that is, members of true Israel. The term *Israel* in this context is a metonymy that refers to the church of Christ. Membership is available to anyone who chooses to trust in Christ. This was God's intention since the days of Abraham (Genesis 22:15-18). Remember—all things, good and bad, work together for good! Leave the motion picture to God; be faithful in your supporting role!

GPS

WHAT'S LOVE GOT TO DO WITH IT?

~ ✲ ~

ROMANS 13:10

*Love does no wrong to a neighbor; therefore
love is the fulfillment of the law.*

Why is love the fulfillment of the law?

Two phrases sum up the Ten Commandments as well as the whole of God's Law: "You shall love the Lord your God with all your heart, and with all your soul, and with all your mind," and "You shall love your neighbor as yourself" (Matthew 22:37,39). Jesus said, "On these two commandments depend the whole Law and the Prophets" (Matthew 22:40). Paul and James both correctly understand the second of these commandments to be a summary of the first (Romans 13:9; Galatians 5:13-14; James 2:8)—loving one's neighbor is necessarily tied to first committing oneself to loving God. Note that in each of these passages the apostles claim that loving one's neighbor is the "fulfillment of the Law."

To Tina Turner's question, "What's love got to do with it?"—to which she implies, "Nothing"—one must assuredly respond, "Everything." Love is the foundation of a healthy and productive society because it guarantees that God is the society's centerpiece and that its citizens act in ways that are consistent with one another's welfare. Paul encouraged the Galatian Christians to love God and walk by the Spirit, the fruit of which is love, joy, peace, patience, kindness, goodness, faithfulness, gentleness, and self-control. Living in the Spirit of God gives people an ability or aptitude to behave in ways that protect rather than threaten society (Galatians 5:16,22-25). These character traits originate in God, allow people to serve each other appropriately, and enable them to fulfill the whole Law of God (Galatians 5:13-14). James equates God's love with impartiality. The message of God is inconsistent with favoritism, which is a violation of the Law (James 2:9). Only through impartiality does one genuinely reflect the mind of God and make available the mercy that those in need require (see James 1:27; 2:13). Impartiality is an expression of love, which fulfills the intent of the Law.

Paul informs the Roman believers that they are to owe no individual anything except love (Romans 13:8). A person should pay his taxes and faithfully make loan payments, but he cannot pay off his debt to love humanity—the love God has bestowed on humanity cannot be equaled (Ephesians 5:1-2; 1 John 4:10-11). Perfect love is the oxygen of heaven, the absence of selfishness (1 John 3:14), and the pursuit of every believer (1 Corinthians 14:1; 16:14). By description, divine love is monogamous, abhors harm to others, obtains possessions honorably, and is content with God's blessing (Romans 13:9; see also 1 Corinthians 13:1-8).

Today's self-serving and emotionally based understanding of love makes Romans 13:10 confusing. The very fact that we do so much that is detrimental to our relationships with God, our spouses, our children, and with our neighbors indicates that we are quite selfish and do not love them as much as we think. Our maturity is measured by our ability to identify and overcome our shortcomings. Our inconsistency in loving others is definitely one of those shortcomings! However, the more like God we become, the more we are able to love. Therefore, the goal of every person is to know and love God more so that his or her neighbors are wronged less—that is, loved more. The focus of God's Law throughout Scripture is to create and develop loving relationships between God and humanity and between human beings. As love accomplishes this, God's Law is being fulfilled.

GPS

1 CORINTHIANS 3:17

If any man destroys the temple of God,
God will destroy him, for the temple of
God is holy, and that is what you are.

How does a man destroy the church?

Selfishness, unfettered ambition, and arrogance are the nemeses menacing the human race. Eighteenth-century theologian and pastor Jonathan Edwards believed that ambition was man's attempt to steal glory from God. Selfishness is at the root of every personal, national, and international conflict and continues to be the primary threat facing the pastors and congregants that comprise the church of Jesus Christ.

The success of each local church is not determined by the charisma of its pastor, the wealth of its congregants, the size and scope of its facilities, or its proud historical association with great pastors. Any individual who associates with a church for any or all of these reasons is complicit in reducing the church to a human enterprise (1 Corinthians 3:4). In such settings, those with a God-given opportunity to serve become opportunists, "humbly" embracing the praise and adulation of their congregants (3:5). The problem is not that a pastor is a fine orator, or that the congregation is blessed with wealth, or that the church's facilities are substantial. The problem is that the church body has neglected or forgotten their redeemed or purchased status. They have become full of themselves rather than full of Him (3:6-9,21-23; 6:19-20)! Selfishness is a subtle intruder that lurks patiently in the heart of every person. If we ignore it or think we have overcome it, it will seep out like a toxic chemical and contaminate the work of God, reducing it to a work of man.

The point is that well-meaning believers can build churches on the foundation of Christ Himself (3:10-11) and then become victims of ambition, simply because they did not overcome their immaturity with thorough and deeper biblical instruction (3:1-3). Sadly, too many churches become shaped by cultural influences rather than by biblical and theological absolutes, especially in Europe and America, where the concept of tolerance has demonized absolutes and become hostile to truth. The efforts of such churches are, according to Paul, as temporal as wood, hay, and straw, which under pressure or heat crumble or burn (3:12-15). Dwelling places of the Spirit of God (Ephesians 2:22)—congregations—established to be pillars of faith, purity, and truth and meant to shape communities are absorbed by them until the gospel of God's saving grace is no longer evident (see Revelation 2–3). Tainting the truth is a hazardous venture. Churches such as these are not dying; they are being *destroyed* by the hand of God, their original and true proprietor (3:16-17). A church whose centerpiece is something other than the triune God no longer possesses the message of grace and mercy and, therefore, is of no good for the souls of humanity or the glory of God.

The church of Christ is holy, set apart from the world for the good of the world. Its only reason for existence is to focus on the Life that gives life. Each believer is responsible for the preservation and presentation of the gospel of Christ for the building up of the saints (Ephesians 4:11-12) and for the sake of those whom He has yet to bring into the fold (2 Timothy 2:10). This is the work of gold, silver, and precious stone that glorifies God, has eternal value, and safeguards the churches.

GPS

1 CORINTHIANS 6:2

*Do you not know that the saints
will judge the world?*

**Do saints or God judge the world, and
when will this judgment happen?**

"He will come again to judge the living and the dead." Those words from the Apostles' Creed, and similar ones from other creeds, have been recited by Christians throughout the centuries who affirmed their belief in God and the basic doctrines of Christianity. No person proclaiming the orthodox tenets of the faith would deny a future judgment by God and Jesus Christ. Yet Paul's words in 1 Corinthians 6:2 add a twist to that belief, indicating that Christians will also participate in a future judgment.

Christians in Corinth struggled with many issues in their culture and within their own fellowship. One of the difficulties was the frequency of disputes between members resulting in lawsuits and legal complaints. Roman society, like our own, was extremely litigious, but Christians suing each other was detrimental to the unity of the church and the survival of the church. Most likely what is in view here are noncriminal property disputes, since Paul teaches elsewhere that criminal cases must be handled by the state (Romans 13:3-4).

As practitioners of a minority religion already suspect by many in the culture, Christians could not afford additional negative public publicity. Therefore Paul encourages them to solve their disputes within the confines of the church body. He then reminds them that they will participate in the future spiritual judgment of the world.

Paul presents this as an indisputable fact, and it was probably one of the things he taught the Corinthians as the congregation was being established several years earlier during his second missionary journey. The point of his reminder is that if Christians are to participate in such an enormous event in the future, surely they can settle daily disputes among themselves.

Many verses teach the participation of believers in future judgment (Daniel 7:22; Matthew 19:28; Revelation 2:26; 3:21; 20:4), and as Paul states in 1 Corinthians 6:3, this will include judgment of the angels (Isaiah 24:21; 2 Peter 2:4; Jude 1:6). This judgment occurs at the end of the millennium (the 1000-year reign of Jesus Christ on earth that follows the rapture, the seven-year Tribulation, and the second coming of Christ). God's prophetic plan includes several future judgments, and the judgment of 1 Corinthians 6:2 probably occurs at the Great White Throne judgment described in Revelation 20:11-15.

This is a good example of the value and importance of prophecy in the life of the Christian. Paul uses a prophetic event to support his teaching about interpersonal relationships and civic practices. Prophecy is not just about the future; it is about the present. If we study, understand, and apply God's Word in daily life, we not only fulfill commands of Scripture, we also grow in our relationship with God and others. Martin Luther wrote that the Bible "is not merely to be repeated or known, but to be lived and felt." That is precisely what Paul is encouraging readers to do in 1 Corinthians 6:2.

TJD

70

BAPTISM FOR THE DEAD

~ ✺ ~

1 CORINTHIANS 15:29

Otherwise, what will those do who are baptized
for the dead? If the dead are not raised at
all, why then are they baptized for them?

What is baptism for the dead?

The apostle Paul's words in this verse have puzzled many readers throughout almost 2000 years of Bible study, and more than 200 solutions have been proposed (though very few remain viable).

The straightforward manner in which Paul addresses this topic shows that he and his readers knew exactly what he was referring to, even though subsequent readers throughout history have been perplexed by the verse. And whatever he means by "baptized for the dead," this verse is only a minor element of his larger teaching in 1 Corinthians 15—an elaborate defense of the resurrection of Jesus Christ and the future resurrection of all Christians.

In this first letter to the Christians at Corinth, Paul addressed various problems in the Corinthian church related to the importance of the physical body once individuals became Christians. Some in the church felt that the physical body was of little importance, and this led them either into licentious practices (6:15-16) or ascetic practices (7:1-17)—feast or famine. Paul corrects both of these extremes and then defends the physical resurrection because some Corinthians evidently had extended their views on the body to deny the physical resurrection of Christians (15:12).

Paul argues that the resurrection of Jesus Christ is the foundation for the future resurrection of Christians (15:1-11), and if Christ has not been raised from the dead, then Christians are foolish and their faith is futile (15:14,17). Finally he declares that if the dead aren't raised, the present life is all there is, and everyone should live accordingly (15:32). Within this extended argument, he mentions baptism for the dead.

What was it? There are two major views. Some believe that Christians in Corinth were undergoing baptism on behalf of dead friends and relatives who were not Christians and that the deceased would mystically receive salvation (a practice that may have originated in nearby pagan religions and then wrongly been brought into the Corinthian church). However, this substitutionary activity, in which baptism supposedly has some benefit toward salvation, is contrary to the Bible's teaching that salvation comes as a result of personal faith alone (Romans 3:28; 10:8-9; Galatians 2:16; Ephesians 2:8-9). There is no proxy faith or salvation. This kind of baptism would be contrary to the Bible's teaching about salvation. Baptism for the benefit of a dead person is unbiblical. Had this indeed been the practice, Paul probably would have not only mentioned it, but also condemned it. This verse is the only mention of such a practice in the New Testament or the first-century church, so it probably was not a widespread activity. History records heretical groups practicing similar activities in the second and third centuries, most likely because of misinterpretations of this verse.

A second and more likely understanding of baptism for the dead is that new converts were being properly baptized because of the prior influence of deceased Christians. In this view "the dead" means "the Christian dead" and the baptism occurs because of rather than on behalf of the deceased. Such an interpretation upholds the thrust of Paul's argument as well as salvation through personal faith alone.

TJD

71

NO PAIN, NO GAIN

~ ❄ ~

2 CORINTHIANS 1:5

*Just as the sufferings of Christ are ours
in abundance, so also our comfort
is abundant through Christ.*

**What are the sufferings of Christ, and
why do we experience them?**

Suffering can include feelings, such as loss of control, sadness or sorrow, fear, anger, rejection, shame, disappointment, grief, guilt, and futility. It can be the prolonged physical pain of an illness or injury or the unrelenting anguish that accompanies prolonged emotional and spiritual stress or discomfort. Though we do not seek suffering, it is an unavoidable consequence of life in a fallen and self-centered world (Genesis 3:7-10,14-19). The rebellious nature of humanity is intrinsic, making suffering predictable. That which was innocent and immortal before the fall of humanity became corrupted and mortal after it. In the eternal kingdom, God will reverse this regrettable state of affairs and eliminate suffering (1 Corinthians 15:50-58; Isaiah 25:8-9; 60:18-22; Revelation 21:3-5). Until then, all suffering is linked to humanity's resistance to the rule of God. However, it is not altogether without value.

Paul is referring to suffering that comes as a result of sharing the gospel of Christ with people who resist it (2 Corinthians 1:7-10). Different beliefs often collide and create tension between people. In an intolerant environment, this can lead to altercations and even oppression. The longer and more threatening the altercations, the greater the suffering among those holding the minority view. Jesus' suffering in the Garden of Gethsemane (Mark 14:32-36) was directly linked to the sinfulness of humanity—He certainly held the minority view—however, His suffering produced the hope of salvation offered to the entire human race. Suffering is generally considered worthwhile if it occurs in defense of a universal or eternal principle. A martyr is honored for suffering and dying for the sake of a principle. Biblical suffering invites God's favor when it mirrors the sufferings of Christ who, while being insulted and rejected, remained faithful to the Judge and Guardian of our souls (1 Peter 2:19-25; 4:12-19).

Regardless of the cause of suffering, each experience with it demands endurance—it can last a few days or it can last a lifetime. This is what makes suffering so daunting. Though medical assistance and sound counsel can alleviate or eliminate some forms of suffering, other forms defy resolution, such as those that are the result of unrelenting persecution. Whatever the cause or length of suffering, the dearest friend of the sufferer is the consoler or comforter—the best being someone who has passed through affliction and offers words and acts of encouragement, shares Scripture, ensures that basic needs are met, and intercedes with God on the sufferer's behalf (2 Corinthians 1:4,6-7,11). In so doing, a comforter reflects the "God of all comfort" (1:3), who through Christ endured the affliction of the cross, securing our victory over death (1 Corinthians 15:55-57; 1 Peter 2:24), through the Father saves us and secures our inheritance in heaven (1 Peter 1:3-5), and through the Spirit prays on our behalf when words cannot express our deepest concerns (Romans 8:26). With God and such friends, we possess an abundance of comfort equal to the task of enduring an abundance of suffering for the cause of Christ.

GPS

72

OIL AND WATER DON'T MIX

~ ✦ ~

2 CORINTHIANS 6:14

Do not be bound together with unbelievers; for what partnership have righteousness and lawlessness, or what fellowship has light with darkness?

What kind of relationship is Paul prohibiting?

This wonderful piece of guidance, when misinterpreted, sadly presses many believers into being proponents of legalistic, separatist, or isolationist attitudes and too often creates division between believers and unbelievers and between believers as well. Its intention is just the opposite: to create relationships that further greater unity among believers and with their God (2 Corinthians 6:16; 13:11; 1 Corinthians 1:10) and delineate the appropriate level of the church's interaction with the world, from which God draws its members (Matthew 28:19; 1 Corinthians 5:9-13).

At the outset, we should note that this passage does not prohibit interaction with unbelievers. If isolation were the focal point, Jesus would not have given the Great Commission, and Paul could not have been called to be the apostle to the nations. Proper behavior, such as feeding the famished and clothing the cold, cannot bring conviction to unbelievers without close and loving interaction (Romans 12:20). Also, Paul was adamant about believing spouses not divorcing their unbelieving spouses who want to remain married (1 Corinthians 7:12-14; see 2 Peter 3.1-2). The visible and doctrinally sound witness of the church *in* the world points to the Light of the world.

Nor does this verse specifically deal with the institution of marriage. However, one would be mistaken to suggest that it should not be applied to it. The words "bound together" can also be translated "unequally yoked" or "mismated." One of Ezra's and Nehemiah's difficult struggles with the returning exiles from Babylon to Jerusalem was their inclination to take marriage partners from the surrounding nations (Ezra 9:1-5; Nehemiah 13:23-31). Such marriages would assimilate God's people with the people of the world and corrupt the image of God with which the nation was entrusted, as is every saint today (1 Thessalonians 2:3-4; 2 Timothy 1:14). God intended marriage to reflect the unity of the triune God. A union that involves spouses of different faiths waters down that unity and makes light of its responsibility to accurately reflect God's love and commitment to others.

To what specifically is Paul referring? In the preceding verses (2 Corinthians 6:11-13), Paul expresses his desire for the Corinthians to be as open in their affections for him as he is for them. However, something is interfering with the Corinthians' ability or willingness to associate more closely and openly with Paul and his entourage. The hearts of the Corinthians are not knit together with Paul's. Rather than being dedicated servants of God (as Paul described in verses 4-10), the believers in the church in Corinth appear to have become dedicated servants of philosophical pluralism by willingly associating with thoughts, practices, and influences of faiths that were inconsistent and incompatible with the gospel of Christ (see 1 Timothy 6:3-5). The church of Jesus Christ is to be one universal, unified body of believers under the authority and protection of the one and only living God (2 Corinthians 6:16). We must understand the philosophy of the unbelieving world and keep it from diluting what the world and the church most need: divine truth. The separation from the world is not so much physical as it is intellectual and relational. No association with the world should remain that dilutes sound doctrine, hinders one's relationship with God, and hampers fellowship between believers (1Timothy 4:6-8; 6:13-15; Hebrews 12:1-3).

GPS

73

GOD CHOSE YOU
~ ❋ ~

EPHESIANS 1:5

He predestined us to adoption as sons
through Jesus Christ to Himself,
according to the kind intention of His will.

What does it mean to be predestined?

Every field of study, academic discipline, and profession has a specialized vocabulary used to accurately articulate and define its subject matter. Whether the topic is chemistry or computers, medicine or music, food or fashion, philosophy or politics, all use unique terms and phrases. Theology and biblical studies are no exceptions. The use of precise words and unfamiliar concepts can be intimidating or bewildering as anyone who has purchased a computer can attest. But such need not be the case, especially in studying the Bible and Christian beliefs.

Predestination is a unique Bible and theology vocabulary word. But it shouldn't be intimidating, and it is very important.

The Bible teaches that God has a complete plan for the universe, and He has made sure that some situations and events of that plan are certain to happen. That certainty touches people's lives and is called *predestination.* The emphasis of predestination and of this verse is more on *what* than *who.* God has predestined Christians to adoption into God's family.

Biblical words like *election, predestination,* and *foreknowledge* all involve some mystery and can be confusing as well as controversial. But that is not the reason they are in the Bible. Each of them is there to encourage humility, confidence, joy, faithfulness, and holy living. They are words of reassurance for believers, who must live in a world filled with difficulty, opposition, and hostility to God.

In this verse, Paul is saying, "Because He predestined us, God chose us." God chose by predestinating. Christians were predestined in eternity past to become adopted sons and daughters of God so that upon conversion they are adopted into the family of God. Since there was no concept of adoption in Judaism, Paul's use of the term in this verse (and four other times in the New Testament) is probably based on the Roman practice that was done primarily to carry on a family name, property, and wealth. Being adopted brought great gain to the adoptee, just as Christians receive salvation, many spiritual benefits, and the full realization of being adopted into God's family at the time of their resurrection in the future (Romans 8:23). There is no greater gain in all of life.

If you are a Christian, you can rejoice and enjoy the certainty of salvation in Jesus Christ. Your sins are forgiven, you have eternal life, and you are part of the family of God.

TJD

74

DOWN AND UP

~ ❈ ~

EPHESIANS 4:9

Now this expression, "He ascended," what
does it mean except that He also had
descended into the lower parts of the earth?

Did Jesus descend into hell?

Belief that Jesus descended into hell after His death and before the resurrection is a common view that has appeared throughout the centuries in various Christian creeds. Most notably, it is included in later versions of the Apostles' Creed. One of the verses cited for support of this teaching is Ephesians 4:9. But the Apostles' Creed was not written by any of the apostles or a single church council. Rather, it was developed during a 500-year period from AD 200 to 750, and the phrase about the descent into hell was incorporated into the statement of faith at a very late date. But is that what Paul had in mind in this passage?

In Ephesians 4, Paul is discussing unity and diversity in the entire church. In 4:8 he summarizes Psalm 68, especially verse 18. This psalm portrays a triumphant warrior returning in glory, receiving gifts, and distributing gifts to his followers. Paul uses that imagery and says that by redeeming sinful people, Jesus Christ provides spiritual liberation and then presents Christians as gifts to the universal church. Each person is unique and has different abilities and responsibilities within Christ's church (Ephesians 4:11-12).

In this context, verses 9-10 provide a parenthetical comment on Jesus' distribution of gifts by stating that before Jesus could ascend into heaven, He first had to descend "into the lower parts of the earth." Just as in a round-trip journey, where a person must leave home before the second part of returning home, so also did Jesus have to leave heaven before returning to heaven.

To where did Christ descend? What did Paul mean by the "lower parts of the earth"? Some have understood this to refer to Christ's descent at Pentecost to give spiritual gifts to the church through the Holy Spirit, but three other major understandings exist. Many have understood the phrase to denote parts lower than the earth or under the earth in support of a descent into Hades. Others believe Paul was saying that Jesus descended to earth, and the phrase should be read "the lower parts, namely, the earth." A third solution is that it refers to the incarnation and subsequent death of Jesus with the idea being "the earth's lower part, the grave."

This latter view fits the immediate context of the passage well. Paul is stating that the same Christ who went up into heaven in His ascension is also He who earlier came down from heaven. He descended from heaven to be born as a human. In His incarnation, He was indeed crucified, He died, and He was buried, gloriously rising on the third day as victor over sin and death, offering spiritual liberation and salvation to all.

TJD

75

GRIEVING THE HOLY SPIRIT

~ ✳ ~

EPHESIANS 4:30

Do not grieve the Holy Spirit of God,
by whom you were sealed for
the day of redemption.

How does a person grieve the Holy Sprit?

Everyone has experienced moments of sorrow and sadness. They occur in times of personal loss, disappointment, or troubling experiences. Grief is an intensely personal emotion that none of us desire. The Bible teaches that all three persons of the Trinity (God the Father, God the Son, and God the Holy Spirit) also experience emotions. One such emotion is grief.

The apostle Paul wrote the New Testament book of Ephesians during a time of Roman imprisonment. In it he repeatedly writes of the importance of the Holy Spirit in daily life and in personal spiritual growth. He also urges his readers to not grieve the Holy Spirit. Such an exhortation raises several questions: What does it mean to grieve the Holy Spirit? How is it done? Why is it wrong? What are the consequences of such an act?

The Holy Spirit is very real and is God. He is not an impersonal force, power, or entity. Because the Holy Spirit is God, He possesses all the divine attributes, such as being all knowing (1 Corinthians 2:10-11), being present everywhere (Psalm 139:7), being all-powerful (Genesis 1:2), and possessing and being all truth (1 John 5:6). The work of the Holy Spirit is multifaceted in the lives of individuals and in the world as a whole (John 16:8-11; Romans 8:14,16; 1 Corinthians 6:19; 12:13; Titus 3:5) and has been since creation.

Because the Spirit is a person, certain acts can be performed or committed toward Him just as might occur against any other person. Among these acts are disobeying (Acts 26:19), lying (Acts 5:3), resisting (Acts 7:51), blaspheming (Matthew 12:31), outraging (Hebrews 10:29), and grieving (Ephesians 4:30).

In the passage in which the apostle Paul tells the Ephesians not to grieve the Holy Spirit, he exhorts them to live a lifestyle that is equal to and worthy of their status as adopted sons and daughters of God because of their salvation (Ephesians 4:1-3). Everyday activities are important and reflect personal values. Spiritually, the Ephesians were not the people they used to be, and therefore they were not to live according to their former ways.

Grieving the Holy Spirit is mentioned once in the Old Testament (Isaiah 63:10) in reference to the rebellion of the Israelites in the wilderness (Exodus 20). In both the Old and New Testaments, the Holy Spirit is grieved or pained when those who are God's own sin. The context of Ephesians 6:6 shows that grieving the Holy Spirit occurs especially when believers speak words of anger, bitterness, slander, and degradation. The childhood taunt "Sticks and stones may break my bones, but words will never hurt me" simply isn't true. Our speech, conversations, and words do matter. They matter to others, but more importantly, they matter to God, for they are audible indicators of the condition of our inner selves. A pure heart yields pure words; an impure heart produces lies and falsehoods and in so doing, grieves the Holy Spirit. This is why King David prayed, "Let the words of my mouth and the meditation of my heart be acceptable in Your sight, O LORD, my rock and my Redeemer" (Psalm 19:14).

                                                            TJD

76

DOWNWARD MOBILITY

~ ❋ ~

PHILIPPIANS 2:7

*[Christ Jesus] emptied Himself, taking
the form of a bond-servant, and being
made in the likeness of men.*

How and of what did Jesus empty Himself?

In our culture we often talk about upward mobility, getting ahead in life—moving up in the world financially and socially. Yet the Bible tells us that Jesus did just the opposite. He literally moved down—from heaven to earth.

Jesus Christ has always existed as the second person of the Trinity (John 1:1; 8:58). Along with God the Father (the first person) and God the Holy Spirit (the third person), Jesus is God. He existed throughout eternity past and all of the Old Testament era. But at the right time in God's plan, He became a man, a real human person (Galatians 4:4). When this happened at His conception and birth, He was fully God and fully man. Amazingly, He did not cease to be God; He was God in human flesh. Christ became human. This is the event that the apostle Paul discusses in Philippians 2:5-11 when he encourages Christians to live a lifestyle of humility, imitating Jesus Christ.

Using the imagery of pouring out a jar, Paul says that Jesus emptied Himself; He divested Himself of something. What? Jesus temporarily emptied Himself of His manner of existence as equal to God. He did not set aside His deity and divine characteristics. Rather, He temporarily left heaven to come to earth and take on human form and die on a cross for the sins of all people.

When Jesus came to earth, He temporarily set aside or surrendered the independent use of His divine powers. When He used His divine attributes He did so only under the control of the Holy Spirit and in accordance with the Father's will.

When Paul says Jesus took the form of servant, the sense of the word *took* is not that Jesus exchanged something, but rather that He added something. He added human personhood alongside His deity. He did not lose His deity, but added His humanity. Jesus added the limitations of humanity and temporarily ceased to use some of His divine prerogatives (Matthew 24:36). God cannot cease to be God, but He can take on additional status. The likeness that Jesus took on means that although He was a genuine man, some aspects of His humanity were not absolutely like other people's. For example, Jesus was fully human, but He did not have a sin nature (Hebrews 4:15).

No one likes to be humbled or humiliated. When we are, we feel insignificant, diminished, belittled, and embarrassed. Yet from a human viewpoint, that is exactly what happened to Jesus. Giving up the status and privileges of heaven, Jesus freely took on human flesh and blood in order to serve all people by dying for them. His humility and condescension to humanity included not only His birth in Bethlehem, but also His crucifixion and death in Jerusalem.

Jesus left the splendor of heaven for the humility of the cross. It is this very thought that the hymn writer Charles Wesley captured so well with the lyrics, "Amazing love! How can it be that Thou, my God, shouldst die for me?"

TJD

PHILIPPIANS 2:12

*My beloved, just as you have always
obeyed, not as in my presence only,
but now much more in my absence,
work out your own salvation
with fear and trembling.*

Who is responsible for a person's
salvation and eternal life?

When Paul told the Philippians to work out their salvation, he did
not mean that they were to work for it or acquire it through their own
efforts. In fact, they were already secure in their belief and salvation
(Philippians 1:1). No one, ourselves included, can work for salvation
because it is a gift from God (Ephesians 2:8-9), but we can work out
our spiritual position (Ephesians 2:10). Salvation involves deliverance
from the penalty and eternal consequences of sin, but every Christian is
responsible for his or her own spiritual development and struggles with
the daily consequences of the sin nature. While the Holy Spirit actively
works in our lives, success or failure is up to us (Romans 8:9,14,16).

Paul commanded the Philippians to put into practice through the
aid of the Holy Spirit the results of the salvation they received from God.
God would enable them to do it (Philippians 2:13), but they needed to
actively pursue the ramifications of having eternal life and the benefits
of living godly lives. Spiritual progress is a cooperative effort between the

Christian and the Holy Spirit. It is an outworking of a person's rebirth as a Christian.

Paul was certain that just as God worked in his life and through him, so too would God work in the Philippians' lives (Philippians 1:6; 4:9). Because of this, they were to be joyful in daily life (as should be all Christians), but they were also to fully understand the enormous responsibility and obligation of serving Jesus Christ. They were (and we are) to serve with "fear and trembling." Being joyful and being fearful might seem to be contradictions, but they are not.

Paul uses the phrase "fear and trembling" several times to indicate a positive emotional response to understanding God's desires for those He loves (1 Corinthians 2:3; 2 Corinthians 7:15; Ephesians 6:5). It is an attitude of obedience and awe rather than fright. To experience God's best in our lives, we must have complete trust in Him and in the unique plan He has for each of us. As we journey with God, we work out our salvation, fully realizing the magnitude of the gift He has given us. In much the same way that the gift of a luxury automobile is fully understood and appreciated only as the new owner drives it, so too is salvation more fully comprehended as a person daily lives according to God's plan and God's Word. Fine automobiles are not meant to stay in the garage, and salvation is not meant to be dormant or static.

TJD

HEAD-OF-THE-LINE PRIVILEGES

~ ❋ ~

COLOSSIANS 1:15

He is the image of the invisible God,
the firstborn of all creation.

> **If Jesus is eternally God, why is**
> **He called "the firstborn"?**

At first glimpse this verse seems to imply that at some point God the Father brought Jesus into existence. And if Jesus was created, was the Holy Spirit as well? In fact, Arius and his followers used this verse and similar ones (John 1:14; 3:16,18; 1 John 4:9) in the early history of the church to teach that there was a time when Jesus did not exist. The Council of Nicea condemned his heresy, called Arianism, in AD 325. Christians have recited and affirmed the Nicene Creed ever since. No inferiority exists within the Trinity. The Father, Son, and Holy Spirit each have no beginning.

According to ancient custom, the firstborn male in a family had unique rights and privileges. Besides an inheritance, these included the right of leadership and authority in the family for that person's generation. The Old Testament story of Esau trading his birthright for a bowl of stew is about the bartering of such privileges (Genesis 25:29-34; Deuteronomy 21:17).

When Paul states that Jesus is "the firstborn of all creation," he is not teaching that there was a time when Jesus did not exist or that Jesus was at some point not divine. The Bible repeatedly emphasizes both the deity and eternality of Jesus (John 1:1; 8:58; 20:28). Although Jesus had a birth as a human being, He was always God. Nor is Paul teaching that Jesus was the first of many gods. Rather, Paul is using the term *firstborn* figuratively to emphasize the unique rule and role of Jesus Christ over all of creation. Jesus Christ is not the firstborn *in* creation, but the firstborn *over* creation. Jesus is not part of creation, but the One who made it. And just as Jesus is the source and head of the created world (Colossians 1:15-17), so too is He the source and head of the universal church (1:18-20). Like two stanzas of a hymn, Paul uses the imagery and parallels of Jesus as firstborn and leader.

The Christians in Colossae, a commercial city about a hundred miles east of Ephesus in present-day Turkey, were struggling with a fusion of legalism, mysticism, and philosophic speculation that was destroying their Christianity and spirituality. In order to combat heretical practices and beliefs, Paul wrote to them emphasizing the supremacy and all-sufficiency of Jesus Christ. In his letter to them he stressed Christ's significance as the Lord of creation and the head of the church, and he emphasized the unity Christians share with Christ because of their belief in His sacrificial death for them.

Pagan mythology commonly postulated the existence of divine children born to the gods and goddesses or of humans who in some way became deities. Such beliefs are still part of many false teachings, religions, and spiritualities in contemporary society. But the Bible clearly and repeatedly rejects such views and warns Christians not to be persuaded by them. Jesus Christ, the unique and eternal Son of God, loves you and died for you on the cross. Don't be fooled by any teaching, whether printed on a bumper sticker or preached over the airwaves, that teaches otherwise.

TJD

COLOSSIANS 2:9

For in Him all the fullness of
Deity dwells in bodily form.

What does "fullness of Deity" mean?

This term is used only here in the Bible, although Paul and other writers use similar phrases and ideas elsewhere (John 1:16; Colossians 1:19).

When Paul wrote to the Colossians, part of his purpose was to refute a teaching called Gnosticism that was influencing some of the Christians at Colossae. According to this pagan belief, all matter was inherently evil, and only the soul and the mind were good. This logically led to a denial of God's creation of the world as well as a denial of Jesus' incarnation or humanity.

Gnostics denied that Jesus was ever human and that Jesus died physically or was literally resurrected from the grave. In this letter, Paul attacks these teachings and argues that Jesus, as God, created the universe (1:16), died on the cross (1:20), and had a human body (2:9). But he adds more, declaring that during His time of humanity, Jesus also retained all the attributes and characteristics of God (see also Philippians 2:5-8).

All the powers and attributes that Jesus possessed in His deity were also present in His humanity. All that God is in His divine essence is present also in Jesus Christ. No inferiority or subordination exists within the Trinity or between God the Father and God the Son. God's loving, merciful, and forgiving nature was manifested and demonstrated by the life and death of Jesus Christ. He was God incarnate, and that is why He said, "He who has seen Me has seen the Father" (John 14:9).

In Colossians 2:9, Paul is doing more than simply teaching a technical or abstract point of theology. He is reminding the Colossian Christians and all who would hear this letter that because Jesus is God and Christians have a unique relationship to Him, they too have received grace and enormous blessings (Colossians 2:10; Ephesians 1:3). The Gnostics promoted a spiritual hierarchy and caste system that required secret knowledge for advancement. They also taught that a person had to work through angels and many intermediaries to have access to God. The Bible rejects these views. The fullness of God is in Jesus Christ, and the Christian is complete in Jesus Christ, who alone serves as a mediator and advocate for all who believe (1 Timothy 2:5). No superiority or inferiority exists among Christians. No one is lesser or greater than another. All Christians are equal (Galatians 3:26-28).

TJD

80

IT'S NOT AN ACCESSORY

~ ❀ ~

1 THESSALONIANS 5:17

Pray without ceasing.

How can someone never stop praying?

This phrase comes in the second of three sets that propose 18 responsibilities or requirements of Christian conduct. The first set looks at the believer's responsibilities to others (1 Thessalonians 5:12-15), the second looks at the believer's responsibilities to him- or herself (verses 16-17), and the third looks at the believer's responsibilities to purity (verses 18-22). The second set encourages the believer to rejoice always, pray ceaselessly, and in everything give thanks to God.

The church throughout the ages has not lived in a fairyland of happily-ever-afters, but in a world that has given it plenty of reason to despair and grieve. In this real world of persecution, disease, and death, Paul asks believers to rise above the fray, and for good reason. The message of hope is not some fantasy we hang on to get by, but an inevitability. It's a promise God Himself made to His children (1 Peter 1:3-5). Those who rejoice while in sorrow (2 Corinthians 6:10) do so because their genuine faith drives them to pray incessantly to Him who conquered death (1 Corinthians 15:55-56) and to thank Him for the simple privilege of having life in Christ, if only for a limited time on this earth (1 Corinthians 15:56; Philippians 1:18-20). Persistent joy, prayer, and thanksgiving in the midst of pleasure or pain produce a life of divine peace (see Philippians 4:4-6) in the believer who is patiently waiting for the coming of the Lord (1 Thessalonians 5:1-11).

Ceaseless prayer cannot refer to praying every moment of every day. Even for the great prayer warriors of the faith, life has other responsibilities that rightfully demand their time and attention: study, work, family, and sleep, to name just a few. Neither can ceaseless prayer be a continual state of mind or an inner attitude—thinking or caring about prayer and actually talking to God are two different things. When Paul speaks of prayer, he is referring to spending time talking with God about the spiritual needs of the saints and *relentlessly* thanking Him for the work He does in their lives. Prayer is a "one on One" conversation between the Giver and recipient of grace.

An analogy with eating may help us understand what Paul means by ceaseless prayer. "Don't stop eating" may mean to finish a meal, but it can also mean to eat every day. To remain healthy, a person must learn to find a balanced diet that is maintained throughout one's life—he must continue eating. Paul just as easily could have said, "Don't stop praying" or "Have a healthy diet of prayer"—a *routine* of some kind. Believers need to be careful not to get so caught up in the affairs of life that they stop talking to God on a regular basis, which, as a guideline, should probably be about as often as one eats. The problem isn't that Christians fail to talk with their Lord daily or even weekly, but that many seldom talk to God for days on end while others only talk to Him when they are struggling or desire something. Would you honestly cease conversing with your spouse or children for days on end? How could we cease to seriously converse with our heavenly Father about eternal issues for weeks or even months on end?

GPS

81

LEAVE IT ON

~ ☀ ~

1 THESSALONIANS 5:19

Do not quench the Spirit.

What does "quench the Spirit" mean?

In 1 Thessalonians 5:19-22, Paul is concerned with purity or sanctification—being set apart from the world to reflect God's will and character. He warns his readers that rejecting God's view of sexual purity is synonymous with rejecting Him and the Holy Spirit, whose function is to guide and instruct believers in truth and godly living (1 Thessalonians 4:7-8; see also Ezekiel 36:27; Nehemiah 9:20; John 14:16-17,26; 15:26; 16:7-13).

Paul reminds the Thessalonians how indispensable the Holy Spirit's ministry is to their spiritual well-being as individuals and as a church body, so he exhorts them: "Stop quenching the Spirit!" The word *quench* can also be translated "extinguish," "put out," or "restrain." Scripture sometimes associates the ministry of the Spirit with fire (Acts 2:3). Putting out this purifying fire does not merely interfere with the Spirit's life-transforming work; *it discontinues it*. Disobedience is a great offense to the indwelling Spirit of God, yet He remains with us and grieves over the selfish behavior that pushes Him away (Ephesians 4:20-30; see Isaiah 63:10-14). To prevent this quenching of the Spirit, Paul suggests a four-point course of action (COA): 1) Don't despise prophetic utterances, 2) examine or test everything for its accuracy, 3) hold fast to that which is good, and 4) abstain from every form of evil (1 Thessalonians 5:20-22).

One ministry of the Holy Spirit is to distribute gifts to each believer (Romans 12:3-8; 1 Corinthians 12:7-11,20-31). Half of the gifts address communicating the word of God publicly, the most desirable during the early years of the church being prophecy, for it brings edification, exhortation, and consolation (1 Corinthians 14:1-4). Early church prophets were important because Scripture was incomplete, and many of the churches did not have access to New Testament writings. The Holy Spirit guided prophets to receive and teach God's word (Acts 13:1-5) as well as predict future events (Acts 11:27-30). Apparently the Thessalonians had seen too many false prophets and had chosen to despise or ignore anyone who thought himself a true prophet, thus effectively eliminating or quenching the work of the Spirit in their midst. The first course of action for avoiding the quenching of the Spirit is to identify and use all of the gifts given by the Spirit to members of the local church. Now that the Word of God is complete, the Holy Spirit may not utilize some of the gifts except in extraordinary situations where He might deem one practicable (such as prophecy or tongues).

Paul was not ignorant of the fact that false teaching and prophets abounded, so he admonished the church to test or examine the trustworthiness of everything (COA 2; 1 Corinthians 12:1-3; 1 Timothy 4:1-5; 1 John 4:1-6; see also Jeremiah 6:27-30). Today, we have the Holy Spirit and the completeness of God's Word to separate what is good from evil. By walking in the Spirit and valuing God's Word, we obtain the fruit of the Spirit and do that which is good and profitable (COA 3; Romans 12:9-18; Galatians 5:16,22-26; Ephesians 5:9; 2 Timothy 3:16-17; James 3:17). But if we choose to misuse our freedom in Christ, we will walk in the flesh, according to our own wishes, and be overcome with all manner of evil (COA 4; Romans 8:6-8; 12:21; Galatians 5:17,19-21; Ephesians 4:25-32). Love, walk with, and appreciate Him, and He will forever remain an unquenchable fire in your soul.

GPS

2 THESSALONIANS 2:3

Let no one in any way deceive you, for it
[the day of the Lord] will not come unless
the apostasy comes first, and the man of
lawlessness is revealed, the son of destruction.

What does "the apostasy" mean?

Thessalonica was a major seaport in Macedonia and a significant commercial and military center in the Roman Empire. When Paul wrote to the Christians there in the summer of AD 51, he did so because of their confusion regarding future events. They were undergoing persecution because of their faith, and they were being exposed to false teaching. As a result, some Christians there had come to equate their experiences with the prophesied events of the "day of the Lord." Thinking they had missed Christ's return, they believed they didn't need to continue to be steadfast in their faith. Paul reassures readers that Jesus has not returned and that although their persecution and suffering is intense, it is not part of the last days.

In 2 Thessalonians 2:1, Paul reminds his readers of a future "gathering together" of Jesus Christ and Christians. This is a reference to the rapture of the church that Paul taught in his earlier letter to these same Christians (1 Thessalonians 4:13-18). In verse 2 he states that he is giving this reminder because of fake communication and false teaching that the Thessalonians received about the day of the Lord (the seven-year

Tribulation). In verse 3 he declares that the Tribulation will follow "the apostasy," which is then followed by the rise and rule of the Antichrist.

The main interpretive issue in the verse is the lexical meaning of "apostasy" in this context. Various Bible translations and theological presentations of the verse have offered little agreement. Four views have emerged through the centuries: 1) Apostasy is a reference to the Antichrist mentioned later in the verse, 2) apostasy refers to a religious defection or falling away from the faith in the last days (by either the professing church, the Jews in the Tribulation, or non-Christians), 3) apostasy refers to an active revolt or rebellion against God, or 4) apostasy refers to the rapture, that is, the departure of the church prior to the coming of the Antichrist and the Tribulation.

The last three views have been most accepted. Certainly elsewhere the Bible clearly warns of a departure from the faith during the last days of the church. Seven major passages alert us against such spiritual desertion (1 Timothy 4:1-3; 2 Timothy 3:1-5; 4:3-4; James 5:1-8; 2 Peter 2; 3:3-6; Jude 1-25). In these passages, apostasy is clearly doctrinal defection, but it is within the semantic range of the word for it to mean a physical departure (rapture) rather than metaphorical departure (rebellion or falling away).

A definitive dogmatic interpretation in 2 Thessalonians 2:3 is unwise because neither view is conclusive. If the more common view of "falling away" or "rebellion" is understood, Paul is saying that doctrinal defection precedes the rise of the Antichrist (which is also confirmed from other verses). If the view is taken that the word refers to the physical rapture of the church, Paul is saying that the rapture occurs prior to the emergence of the Antichrist (also taught elsewhere). Either view upholds a rapture followed by the Antichrist and the Tribulation.

The important truth Paul is upholding is that Christians (either in his day or today) have not missed the rapture or the second coming of Christ (after the rapture and Tribulation). Therein is comfort and hope regardless of one's circumstances.

TJD

PULLING YOUR WEIGHT

~ ❀ ~

2 THESSALONIANS 3:10

If anyone is not willing to work,
then he is not to eat, either.

How can a good God intentionally
deny food to a hungry person?

The prevailing attitude in America toward the poor is all-inclusive, that is, the poor deserve the assistance of the more prosperous citizens regardless of the reason or cause for their impoverished state. America's immediate response to the poor who were displaced by hurricane Katrina in September of 2005 testifies to this widespread attitude. Without knowing how the money was going to be used or how much was actually needed, Americans sent millions of dollars to Katrina funds all over the nation. Evidence of misuse emerged when the federal government issued $2000 in cash to the victims. Within days, multiple stories began to surface of needy victims using the money to purchase alcohol, cigarettes, and pornography.

Poor and low-income people live in communities throughout the world for many reasons (Matthew 26:11). The needs of most are legitimate, and we should meet them. Doing so is an example of true faith (James 1:27; 2:14-16). However, some are destitute because they refuse to work. They know that an organization or government program will inevitably come to their aid. Paul is referring to people such as these, especially in the church. If a person can work, but is too lazy or self-centered to do what is required to make ends meet, then he should be denied assistance. These people intentionally live unruly and undisciplined lives (2 Thessalonians 3:6-7,11). They are sluggards who crave everything, but they do next to nothing to acquire it (Proverbs 13:4; 6:6-11). Those who assist these folks mistakenly feed their weakness more than their bellies—an act that does nothing to help them in the long run. Such assistance is therefore unloving.

Alexander Hamilton understood this principle. When an artist he knew, Ralph Earl, fell on self-imposed hard times and was unable to pay his debts, he was placed in a debtor's prison. Rather than simply pay off the man's debt, Hamilton devised a scheme to assist Earl to earn the money for himself and salvage his dignity. Because Earl was a painter, Hamilton encouraged his wife, Elizabeth, who encouraged others to sit for portraits. Earl's commission eliminated his debt, and he earned his freedom.

The Christian work ethic encourages believers to be industrious and selfless. To refuse to work is frowned upon and a poor example of faith (James 2:17). Paul was unwilling to take from any of the churches without giving something in return. In Thessalonica, Paul and his associates paid for their necessities by working day and night so as not to be a burden on the church. He wanted to be a model of hard work, selflessness, and stick-to-it-iveness.

One should never "become weary of doing good," a worthy exercise which cannot be accomplished without a sound work ethic (2 Thessalonians 3:5,7,11,13). The church or a nation should not waste their resources on the lazy or selfish; they should use those resources to help those whose need is genuine and pressing or long-term. Good hard work is commendable, as is working hard for the good of others who cannot help themselves, which is the same as serving the Lord Himself (Matthew 25:34-40).

GPS

84

FRUIT OF THE VINE

~ ❀ ~

1 TIMOTHY 5:23

No longer drink water exclusively, but
use a little wine for the sake of your
stomach and frequent ailments.

Are Christians permitted to drink wine?

Paul's previous exhortation to Timothy, "Keep yourself free from sin" (1 Timothy 5:22) seems to have triggered a memory of a related issue he wanted to handle parenthetically. Being concerned about Timothy's health, Paul informs him that taking a little wine may help him handle or eliminate some of his "frequent ailments." Some argue that this passage is not an authorization for the general consumption of alcohol, but only for its medicinal use. Many drugs are generally taboo, but as prescriptions they provide protection and relief from numerous ailments. Few people disagree with such a use.

Tea and coffee weren't staples in Europe till the mid-seventeenth century, and then they were consumed only sparingly because sanitation among communities was so poor. Dysentery—the body's uncomfortable response to unwanted parasites and bacteria in the digestive system— occurs when a water supply is contaminated by human feces. Today, more than 700,000 people die every year around the world from amebic or bacillary dysentery. To avoid or diminish this threat, alcoholic beverages are necessarily substituted for water. Alcohol has been known to prolong life, protect the heart, heal baldness, kill lice and fleas, cure exhaustion, ease toothaches, heal canker sores, aid digestion and increase the appetite, remedy yellow jaundice, fight gout, ease pain in swollen breasts, and cleanse wounds.

Clearly, 1 Timothy 5:23 permits the medicinal use of alcohol; nonetheless, we cannot conclude that this is its only appropriate use. To ease Timothy's mind about using alcohol medicinally, Paul reminds Timothy about something he had previously written to him: "For everything created by God is good, and nothing is to be rejected, if it is received with gratitude; for it is sanctified by means of the word of God and prayer" (4:4-5).

Christians must take an honest look at Scripture regarding the use and consumption of alcohol. Many in the church resist even the slightest association with it, but they do so on cultural grounds rather than on any sound biblical prohibition. The position of Scripture on alcohol is similar to positions taken by civilized nations throughout world history: moderation. The Scripture is concerned about what controls us and therefore strictly prohibits the abuse of any substance that would inhibit the work of the Holy Spirit in our lives (Ephesians 5:18).

Though one might justifiably refrain from drinking beer for cultural reasons—it is associated with sexual promiscuity, drunkenness, and carousing—the problem is not with the beer itself, it is with the cultural relationship. Such a position is arguable (see Romans 14). However, excess is the real problem (Proverbs 20:1; 23:20,29-30; Ecclesiastes 10:17; Isaiah 5:11; 28:1; Habakkuk 2:15; Luke 21:34; Romans 13:13; 1 Corinthians 6:10; Galatians 5:21; 1 Peter 4:3).

Many people drink various kinds of alcohol responsibly and should not be viewed as sinful, unspiritual, or unchristian. Some consume alcohol in modest amounts because it is thought to thin the blood and protect the heart. We need to be more biblical in our positions and much less emotional—a proper witness of the gospel requires no less.

GPS

85

DEALING WITH DOLLARS

~ ❋ ~

1 TIMOTHY 6:10

The love of money is a root of all sorts
of evil, and some by longing for it have
wandered away from the faith and
pierced themselves with many griefs.

Should Christians avoid wealth?

Okay, everybody pull out of the stock market as fast as you can, and be sure that you don't open any interest-bearing CDs or checking and saving accounts. And by the way, all credit cards and debit cards have to go! The potential for their misuse is too great.

This attitude is not that different from the attitudes of Thomas Jefferson and James Madison when they fought tenaciously to prevent Treasury Secretary Alexander Hamilton from establishing a government bank. They properly saw the mischief that can occur when people sense a windfall in wealth, but their minds were closed to the honest benefits that a bank could bring to average citizens just trying to run a business in the black. Humans are indeed a selfish and greedy lot, but refusing to seek a good end simply because someone with few scruples might take advantage of it seems a bit narrow-minded and harmful. Banks and the money they secure and move are essential to a healthy economy and are foundational to a people's quality of life. Money itself is not evil.

Capitalism, for all its treasured benefits, has at least one undeniable and threatening shortcoming: the potential for greed. This greed (or lust) for money or wealth subordinates prudence and sound principles. It places self-interest over the interests of others, and it makes lasting and desirable traits like peace and contentment inferior to personal prosperity and power. The safety net of any capitalist society is for its national interests to supersede the personal and self-interests of its citizens. Since this requires selflessness and people are naturally self-centered, it has and will always create a tug-of-war. Selflessness leads to faith, godliness, righteousness, love, endurance, gentleness, peace, and contentment (1 Timothy 6:6-8,11); greed leads to suspicion, ruin of the family, prison, prenuptial agreements, perjury, theft, murder, war, and eternal loss of some kind (1 Timothy 6:9; see Ecclesiastes 5:10-14; Jeremiah 17:11; James 5:1-3).

God is not opposed to hard work (Ecclesiastes 5:12) and wise and sensible investments that produce wealth. Personal wealth among believers benefits the church and its less fortunate members, and it is a reflection of God's blessing, not humankind's genius (1 Timothy 6:17-18). The Lord's concern is with those who would risk the pursuit of their faith and its lasting benefits (1 Timothy 6:13-17; Hebrews 11:26) for temporal profits that only have worth this side of the grave (1 Timothy 6:7; Job 1:21; Psalms 49:10; Proverbs 23:5; 27:24). "What is the advantage to him who toils for the wind?" (Ecclesiastes 5:15-16). Temporal goals and achievements must never replace one's quest for eternal treasures, which offer substantial benefits for self and others on both sides of the grave (1 Timothy 6:19; Proverbs 8:18).

Establishing IRAs, investing in companies, opening annuities, purchasing CDs, and opening interest-bearing saving and checking accounts are all wise choices. Use responsibly and generously that with which God blesses you (1 Timothy 6:18; Luke 12:33); however, never place personal prosperity above personal faith, for your mind will tenaciously pursue what your heart treasures (Matthew 6:19-21). Be content with the progress of your earthly status; remain discontented only with the progress of your heavenly status.

GPS

86

YOU DIDN'T DO IT

~ ❋ ~

TITUS 3:5

*He saved us, not on the basis of deeds
which we have done in righteousness, but
according to His mercy, by the washing of
regeneration and renewing by the Holy Spirit.*

How did we become so wonderfully saved?

This age-old question, when understood, opens up a whole new world of appreciation for God and His truly amazing grace.

Moses' desire to see the Lord's glory resulted in what we might call a preview. God, unwilling to harm Moses with a full display of His glory, grants him only what Moses can endure without losing his life (Exodus 33:20; Job 9:11; 23:8; 1 Timothy 6:16; 1 John 4:12). He permits Moses to see only His goodness and lovingkindness, as revealed in this statement; "I will be gracious to whom I will be gracious, and will show compassion on whom I will show compassion" (Exodus 33:19). A fuller explanation of this preview (Exodus 34:6-7; see also Romans 9:15, where the word *mercy* is an equivalent of *gracious*) clearly shows that God's goodness is expressed through His grace, kindness, and mercy—the same qualities Paul uses to explain how God is moved to save human beings (Titus 3:4-5). Humanity's hopeless and unrighteous state moves God's inherent goodness to reach out and offer to humanity what we are incapable of achieving: the eternal salvation of our souls. With His mercy, everything (Titus 3:8; 1 Peter 1:3-5); without it, nothing (Titus 3:3; 2:11-14)!

His goodness (or more specifically, His mercy) saves us through two aspects of the Holy Spirit's work: an initial spiritual washing or awakening through regeneration (justification) and our subsequent daily transformation through renewal (sanctification).

Our natural bent toward self-glorification (Genesis 2:17; 3:1-7) creates within us an obstinacy and hostility toward spiritual things (Exodus 32:9; 2 Chronicles 24:19; Acts 7:51; Romans 8:7-8). We are like impenetrable stones that are spiritually cold (dead), wanting nothing to do with God. But God is a lover of life and the one who plans and pursues humanity's remedy (Titus 3:4; 2 Samuel 14:14; Ephesians 2:5; 1 John 4:10). Just as He has made and will yet make the impenetrable, obstinate, and wayward heart of Israel penetrable, receptive, and upright (Ezekiel 36:24-27; Romans 11), so through Christ's death, burial, and resurrection and the regenerating work of the Holy Spirit, He brings warmth and life to the cold hearts of the walking dead (Titus 3:5-6; John 1:13; 6:53; 1 Corinthians 6:11; 2 Corinthians 5:17; Ephesians 2:1-7,18). Through His Spirit, God opens our hearts to the truth and salvation, which draw us back to God and into a relationship of His making, not ours.

The moment this relationship is sealed (Ephesians 1:13), the Holy Spirit begins to transform or renew us through the life-changing power of God's Word (Romans 1:16; Ephesians 6:17; Hebrews 4:12). Day after day, the Word chips away at the selfish nature that once kept us from God to create a heart that is no longer contentious, self-centered, full of malice and envy, or easily deceived by foolish teachings and controversies (Titus 3:3,9; Romans 12:1-2; Ephesians 4:17-30; Colossians 3:9-11; Hebrews 12:1-3). Through the renewing work of the Spirit, God's goodness, which saves us, is observable through the good deeds of God's grateful children (Ephesians 2:10; Titus 1:8; 2:7,14; 3:1,8,14). Regeneration gives us spiritual life; renewal teaches us how to live it!

GPS

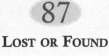
HEBREWS 6:4-6

*In the case of those who have once been
enlightened and have tasted of the heavenly gift
and have been made partakers of the Holy Spirit,
and have tasted the good word of God and the
powers of the age to come, and then have fallen
away, it is impossible to renew them again to
repentance, since they again crucify to themselves
the Son of God and put him to open shame.*

Can believers fall away?

This amazing sentence introduces a warning that has perplexed students of Scripture for centuries. The major debate revolves around the issue of the permanence of salvation. Can a person embrace the gospel of grace and then commit a sin for which he cannot repent? The answer according to this passage is clearly yes. But does the impossibility of repentance prevent a Christian from renewing fellowship that was severed by the falling away, or does the sin wipe out the work of salvation that God has undertaken in the heart of the person?

The latter position simply does not square with the biblical data on the security of the believer. Salvation is a work of God that He promises to complete in each of His children (John 6:37; 10:25-29; Romans 8:1,31-38; 1 Corinthians 3:15; Ephesians 1:13; Philippians 1:6; Hebrews 6:19; 1 Peter 1:3-5; 1 John 5:11-12). The writer of Hebrews is clearly referring to Christian converts from Judaism who he fears are not maturing at a

healthy rate spiritually (Hebrews 5:11–6:3). He fears that their unwillingness to seek a deeper and more meaningful faith will leave them vulnerable
to doctrines that are contrary to truth and may lead to apostasy—the act
of falling away from one's faith to embrace another.

We look at people who have fallen away in two ways. First, some
people are influenced by Christian teachings, warm up to them, and profess commitment to their message without making a genuine confession
of faith. When, for one reason or another, they become discontent or
disagreeable with the faith, they pursue another faith, which denies the
teaching of Christ and leaves them without a means of repentance and
salvation. These folks profess to be Christians but are not (see 1 Samuel
3:14). Hebrews 6 does not refer to these individuals.

Second, some people make a *genuine* confession of faith, do well with
the basic teachings of Christianity (Hebrews 5:12; 6:1-3), benefit from
the work of the Spirit in their lives, enjoy fellowship with God and others,
and experience life as it should be lived apart from the debilitating effect
of sin (6:4-5), but only on a limited level because they do not delve into
the deeper issues of faith. In fact, they may begin to believe that certain
aspects of Christianity are too rigid, exclusive, or generally unacceptable.
In time, they make choices that diminish the work of the Holy Spirit in
their lives (Ephesians 4:30; 1 Thessalonians 5:19) and open themselves
to corruptive teachings that are incompatible with Christianity. These
genuine believers eventually forsake the gift they have been given and fall
into apostasy (false beliefs). With their commitment to Christ severed,
they no longer possess or adhere to the knowledge that enables them
to repent (change their mind) about their inappropriate behavior. Their
redeemed hearts become hardened. The problem is not that God is
unwilling to welcome repentance and renewed fellowship, but that their
corrupted state of mind prohibits them from repenting and returning
to the practice of their faith. These are Christians whose belief systems
belie the grace that secures their souls. A lack or rejection of biblical
knowledge can lead a believer to an apostasy (but not a loss of salvation)
from which he or she cannot return.

GPS

88

A WORKING FAITH

~ ❋ ~

JAMES 2:26

*For just as the body without the spirit is
dead, so also faith without works is dead.*

Does James teach that a person is saved
by good works or by faith alone?

No one argues whether good works are important—they are the behaviors that define the Christian life! The argument is over whether they have any redemptive and saving quality. James 2:14-26 provides much of the kindling in this heated debate by stating that "faith without works is dead" or useless (2:17,20,26) and that a person is "justified by works and not by faith alone" (2:24). Paul, on the other hand, leaves no doubt in his reader's minds that salvation is a gift from God given by grace and accepted through faith. He highlights the fact that salvation is acquired "not as a result of works, so that no one may boast" (Ephesians 2:8-9; see also Romans 3:28; 10:9,13; 2 Timothy 3:15; Titus 2:11; 3:5).

Are Paul and James at odds theologically? Of course not. Paul is discussing the manner in which a person comes to faith—saving faith *precedes* work. James, on the other hand, is discussing how genuinely saved persons behave—works are a *proof* of faith. Both Paul and James use Abraham to support their arguments (Romans 4:3; James 2:23; see Genesis 15:6). Paul argues that Abraham put his faith in Jehovah God—the only one who is capable of justifying the ungodly—and that God rewarded his belief with righteousness. James, on the other hand, uses Abraham's willingness to obey God and sacrifice his son, Isaac

(Genesis 22:2), as evidence that the righteousness he had received from God was genuine. Note that Abraham's act of obedience (Genesis 22:2) comes after his belief in Jehovah produced righteousness (Genesis 15:6). Paul's emphasis is on the Giver of righteousness, while James' is on what righteousness should produce: good and charitable deeds, as Abraham and Rahab illustrate.

Paul and James are not only looking at righteousness from different perspectives, they are also looking differently at faith. James is confronting people who see faith as one-dimensional, a belief in an aspect of God: "You believe that God is one." Good for you; so do demons (James 2:19). Society is inundated with people who believe in God but see Him as or allow Him to become secondary to their other interests. Such faith is useless (2:20). Paul, on the other hand, describes faith as James wants his readers to understand it: an explicit oral and open commitment to Christ as Lord; a heartfelt belief in His death, burial, and resurrection that results in righteousness and salvation (Romans 10:9-10). People with such faith will endure tribulation (1:2-6), pursue righteousness and help families who have lost their providers (1:27), make available a place of worship that is free of favoritism (2:1-13), and clothe and feed their neighbors (2:14-15).

Paul and James also use the words *justify* or *declare righteous* differently. Paul uses the word to describe what God, through faith, does to repentant sinners—He makes them righteous (Romans 4:5; 5:1; 8:33; Galatians 3:24). James uses the word to describe what believers' work evidences—their work shows or proves their righteous standing before God (James 2:21,24-25). By faith, an unbeliever is *made* righteous; by works, a believer is *shown to be* righteous. Works are to faith what breath is to our bodies (2:26). One cannot exist without the other. This is James' point. "I will show you my faith by my works" (2:18). Works are a natural corollary of faith—they are the breath of faith.

GPS

89

So Help Me God

JAMES 5:12

Do not swear, either by heaven or by earth or with any oath; but your yes is to be yes, and your no, no; so that you may not fall under judgment.

What's the big deal with oaths?

Be patient, strengthen your heart, and do not complain about one another, but above all, "your yes is to be yes, and your no, no" until the Lord returns (James 5:7-12). What does this simple construction mean, and why does it carry so much weight in light of the Lord's return? One certainly wants to avoid doing something that results in divine censure.

Oaths are a fairly normal aspect of everyday life. In courtrooms, Americans have historically placed their hand on the Bible and sworn an oath to tell the truth, with God's help. Military officers, upon being commissioned by the president of the United States, swear to defend the Constitution of the United States against all enemies, foreign and domestic. The president of the United States takes a similar oath at his inauguration. These oaths are performed to remind individuals that they are embarking on a grave responsibility that must remain above criticism and that demands the highest degree of integrity. Simply, oaths remind us of the seriousness of something.

James' thoughts are taken from the mind of Jesus (Matthew 5:37). The Lord recalls the seriousness of vows to His audience. "You have heard that the ancients were told, 'You shall not make false vows, but shall fulfill your vows to the Lord'" (Matthew 5:33; Leviticus 19:12).

Dishonesty is equal to insolence; an affront to the very person of God and a violation of the third commandment: "You shall not take the name of the LORD your God in vain" (Exodus 20:7). Jesus raises the standard: "But I say to you, make no oath at all" (Matthew 5:34). Why? Jesus is emphasizing the importance of integrity, which for a believer goes without saying—a child of God doesn't need to swear to anything because telling the truth should be second nature. His yes is yes and his no, no.

Believers do not have to swear by anything—not by heaven, the earth, the Bible, or anything else simply because they are always testifying or proclaiming the truths of God in His very presence (Matthew 5:34-35). When a believer opens her mouth, she is not just talking to those before her; she is speaking before an ever-present God, who is paying close attention to the way she handles the truth. An earthly courtroom is by no means more intimidating than God's courtroom, which, by the way, is always in session.

The simple requirement of an oath says volumes about the natural problem human beings have: The truth too often remains on the tips of our tongues. People insist by means of an oath that their words are true because the veracity of what they have said, or are about to say, may be in doubt. A person who can't be believed without an oath is one who can't be believed with an oath. The truth is a matter of character and theological soundness. Anything short of the truth is the work of the evil one and worthy of divine retribution (James 5:9,12; Matthew 5:37).

With the perseverance of Job, seek the truth; with the patient endurance of the prophets, proclaim the truth, and you will be blessed by God at His coming (James 5:10-11). The believer's duty is to represent God without compromising humanity's deepest need—the truth. As the farmer patiently waits through the season to reap the greatest harvest, so each believer must serve faithfully, often with endurance when troubles come, but always with integrity until the Lord comes (5:7-9). Tell the whole truth and nothing but the truth (2 Timothy 1:13). If God is my witness, no oath is necessary!

GPS

SICK AND TIRED

~ ❋ ~

JAMES 5:14

*Is anyone among you sick? Then he must
call for the elders of the church and they
are to pray over him, anointing him
with oil in the name of the Lord.*

> **Does this book, dedicated to spiritual strength and
> well-being, conclude with a passage that gives
> precise procedures for overcoming physical illness?**

James encourages his readers to find joy in the midst of trials and
testing (James 1:2-4,12), to suppress selfishness through obedience to
God and service to people in need (1:21-27), to avoid the natural desire
to accommodate the upper classes in society at the expense of the less
fortunate (2:1-13), to express faith through good deeds (2:14-26), to know
that teaching requires self-control, as evidenced by the degree to which
one uses his words to edify or efface God and others (3:2,9-10), to strive
for divine wisdom, which leads to greater righteousness (3:17-18), to seek
humility in every aspect of one's life (4:1-17), to pursue the incorruptible
riches of God over the corruptible riches of this world (5:1-6), and to
remain firm in faith and strong of heart until the Lord's return (5:7-12).
"Is anyone among you suffering? Then he must pray. Is anyone cheerful?
He is to sing praises. Is anyone among you sick [weary]? Then he must
call for the elders" (5:13-14).

The greatest threat to believers engaged in spiritual warfare is not
physical sickness; rather, it is weakness of faith or weariness of heart

(discouragement) that makes one susceptible to temptation, sin, and death (1:13-16). James is not talking about sickness and physical healing; he is describing a foolproof procedure for overcoming weakness while engaged in spiritual warfare: Get elder help!

The entire context of this passage soundly argues for spiritual healing and against physical healing. The proper translation of two Greek words, incorrectly translated "sick" in verses 14 *(astheneo)* and 15 *(kamno)*, puts the passage and its meaning into clearer focus and helps us avoid the pitfall of embracing an interpretation that provides false hope to millions who struggle with disease and its debilitating effects. Nowhere in the epistles is a formula even remotely similar to what James is accused of promoting ever used by elders or suggested by an apostle to obligate God to physically heal a person. Paul didn't suggest that Epaphroditus (Philippians 2:25) or Trophimus, whom Paul left sick in Miletus (2 Timothy 4:20), call for the church elders to anoint them with oil and pray for them so as to obligate God's hand in their healing. Nor did Paul seek such a formula to alleviate his own physical affliction (2 Corinthians 12:7-10). In fact, Scripture views physical adversity as temporary and essential to our spiritual maturity (Job 1–2; Romans 8:18; 2 Corinthians 4:16-18; 12:9-10).

Astheneo appears no less than 34 times in the New Testament. In the Gospels, it clearly refers to physical sickness. However, from then on it refers to spiritual weakness or weariness, except when used in reference to Epaphroditus and Trophimus (see above). That James' use of *astheneo* refers to weakness in verse 14 is seen by his use of *kamno* in verse 15. *Kamno* is used only here and in Hebrews 12:3. Although the word can be used to refer to sickness, it is predominantly used to describe weariness. The writer of Hebrews uses *kamno* exactly as does James: We focus on the life, struggles, and victory of Jesus so that we may not "grow weary and lose heart" (Hebrews 12:3). Involving our spiritual teachers (elders) in the daily aspects of our spiritual lives is necessary for building a more mature and unified body of believers. God will always answer prayers that seek divine wisdom, spiritual acumen, and unity. Bank on it!

GPS

JAMES 5:19-20

My brethren, if any among you strays from the
truth, and one turns him back, let him know
that he who turns a sinner from the error
of his way will save his soul from death.

Are fellow believers in jeopardy of spiritual death?

James admonishes believers (James 1:19) to accept trials as tools that hone maturity (1:1-12), not to blame God for their sinful leanings (1:13-17), to put aside behavior that is inconsistent with righteousness (1:21), to avoid favoritism (2:1-13), to avoid falling into the deception that faith is the absence of good deeds (2:14-26), to avoid possessing a loose tongue (3:1-12), to shun jealousy and selfish ambition (3:16), to sidestep lust through humility and submission to the will of God (4:1-17), to choose heavenly riches over earthly gain (5:1-6), and to protect one another from spiritual weariness through effectual prayer (5:7-18). James is exhorting believers to avoid or overcome sinful behaviors. But does James suggest that failure to overcome such behaviors can result in eternal condemnation or spiritual death; that is, the loss of one's salvation?

Death is eternal separation from God (spiritual death) or separation from the body (physical death). The fact that Christians are always growing in spiritual maturity and daily struggle with the "old self," argues against the interpretation that some additional sin will result in spiritual death or eternal damnation, though certainly one's fellowship with God and others is weakened, often significantly. The Bible is clear: eternal condemnation of a

Christian is impossible (Romans 8:1). "If Christ is in you, though the body is dead because of sin, yet the spirit is alive because of righteousness" (Romans 8:10). Eternal life is an unconditional benefit of being in Christ!

The Greek word *psyche* is translated variously to refer to the soul, person, life (physical), or self (one's innermost being). The point to consider is that *psyche* is used to refer to both spiritual and physical death. When Jesus predicted His death, Peter vowed to "lay down my life [soul] for you" to prevent such a thing (John 13:37). Was Peter suggesting that he was willing to have his soul eternally damned? Hardly! He was declaring his willingness to die physically for the Lord. The apostle Paul asked the believers in Philippi to receive and hold in high regard Epaphroditus "because he came close to death for the work of Christ, risking his life [soul] to complete what was deficient in your service to me" (Philippians 2:30). Is Paul insinuating that risking one's life for Christ could lead to eternal condemnation? Unthinkable! Epaphroditus was willing to serve Christ to the point of sacrificing his physical existence. So, it is consistent to suggest that James is referring to saving a person from physical death in 5:20. In James' only other use of *psyche*, he refers to spiritual maturity ("receive the word implanted, which is able to save your souls"—1:21), not specifically to spiritual or physical death although spiritual maturity can prolong a person's physical existence.

Believers who take lightly their responsibility to mature spiritually are susceptible to temptations and failings that more knowledgeable believers can avoid. They also find suffering for the Lord insufferable. Lacking spiritual understanding, they lack patience and endurance (5:7-11). The consequence of such immaturity is falling away (Hebrews 6:4-6), which is accompanied by sinful behavior, weariness, risky behavior and illness that can lead to accidental death (James 5:13-16), or even death as a divine punishment (see 1 John 5:16). The effects of sin are physically and spiritually debilitating. Therefore, believers (lifesavers) are responsible to and for one another. Through intercessory prayer, interaction, and instruction, we can help turn those who, through ignorance or intent, engage in risky sinful behaviors. An effective church body ensures that its members know the Word of God and apply it broadly. Such involvement produces an abiding fellowship with God (James 1:21) and limits sinful behaviors, which might lead to a premature death (5:20).

GPS

NO SECOND CHANCE

~ ❋ ~

1 PETER 3:19

*He [Jesus] went and made proclamation
to the spirits now in prison.*

When did Jesus preach to spirits in
prison, and who were they?

Peter's words about the preaching of Jesus are found in an extended passage (1 Peter 3:13–4:19) on the meaning and purpose of suffering in the lives of Christians. In these verses Peter reminds readers of the suffering of Jesus Christ in His undeserved death and the results that came from that death. The cross was not a defeat but a spiritual victory that brought salvation to all who believe. Through His death and resurrection, Jesus was triumphant over sin, death, and Satan. Moreover, nothing can come against Christians that is beyond the power and control of Jesus Christ (3:22).

Jesus' triumph in the crucifixion and resurrection is certain and not in question. What has been debated through the centuries is when and how Jesus made proclamation to spirits in prison. Even the reformer Martin Luther struggled with this verse's exact meaning, finding it to be strange and obscure.

One common view is that associated with the Apostles' Creed (but not the longer and more detailed Nicene Creed) in the words "he descended into hell," which understands that between the crucifixion and resurrection Jesus preached to imprisoned spirits in hell. These spirits are understood to have been either fallen angels, perhaps from Genesis 6, or humans from the time of Noah or other Old Testament times, who are awaiting the final judgment of God at the end of this age. Often this proclamation is then viewed to have been one of condemnation in which Jesus said in effect, "I told you so!" and announced His victory over sin and death. Also associated with this view but taking a different interpretive tack is an understanding of a second chance at salvation after death (though verse 20 limits the audience to those of Noah's day). Though this passage is often cited in support of such a descent, we do not find the passage to teach such an activity (see also the comments on Ephesians 4:9). Nor is there any support in the Bible for a second chance at salvation after death (Hebrews 9:27).

A second view is that Jesus proclaimed His victory to fallen angels—not between His death and resurrection but at the time (unrecorded) of His ascension into heaven (Acts 1:9). There was a strong tradition and belief within Judaism during the New Testament era of fallen angels being kept in prison (see for example, the extra-biblical book 1 Enoch 10-16,21). While there was a lot of interest in angels during Jesus' day, there is no certainty that Peter's readers were aware of the writing and tradition of 1 Enoch.

A third major view with a long history of support, including Augustine, Aquinas, and many during the Reformation, is that the pre-incarnate Christ preached through Noah to his generation. In this understanding, the preaching was done by Christ through the Holy Spirit and the person of Noah. Just as the Holy Spirit spoke through King David in his day (Acts 1:16; 4:25), so too did it happen in Noah's day while he was building the ark before the great flood. The Spirit preached repentance to the unbelievers of Noah's generation who refused to repent and are now in hell. The view also fits well with 1 Peter 1:10-11, which speaks of the preincarnate Christ speaking through the Old Testament prophets. One shortcoming of this view is that "spirit" is almost never used in the New Testament in reference to people. None of the interpretations is fully satisfactory, and each has grammatical, lexical, or theological shortfalls, though the third view seems most consistent with the immediate context.

What is certain is that Jesus' resurrection was confirmation of all that was prophesied in the Old Testament and that Jesus Christ "is at the right hand of God, having gone into heaven, after angels and authorities and powers had been subjected to Him" (James 3:22).

TJD

1 PETER 3:21

*Corresponding to that, baptism now saves
you—not the removal of dirt from the flesh,
but an appeal to God for a good conscience—
through the resurrection of Jesus Christ.*

Is Peter promoting the idea that baptism, along with faith, saves people?

The context suggests otherwise (see 1 Peter 2:13-20, which refers to patiently enduring mistreatment for doing what is right). Peter is using baptism metaphorically to depict the fullness of faith and to motivate saints to sustain a good conscience by not succumbing to unsolicited suffering.

Baptism is a public expression made mostly in the presence of believers. It is initiated by a private moment that occurs between God and a repentant sinner who, through faith, graciously receives eternal redemption. It is a symbol of faith in God through Christ the Savior and Redeemer, and it is a public testimony of one's lifelong commitment to strive for selfless living in a selfish world.

Water baptism no more saves a person than the waters of the flood saved Noah. In fact, water symbolizes the threat of death. Noah was saved from or out of the water in an ark that he built by faith. His faith in God saved him just as faith in God has saved and will continue to save every person who believes. Baptism in water symbolizes being buried with Christ (dead to sin); being raised from the water symbolizes our resurrection with Him to everlasting life (see Romans 6:1-7; Colossians 2:12). By faith Noah built an ark; by faith we identify with Christ through baptism. Both Noah and all who trust in Christ are saved from the water through faith alone, which saves the soul. Baptism, then, is a post-faith act of obedience done in public to portray the reception of faith (Mark 16:16; Acts 2:38). Spirit baptism also does not save. It too is an outcome of faith, though it takes place in close proximity to saving faith (John 3:5; 1 Corinthians 12:13; Ephesians 1:13-14).

Note that Peter is not trying to evangelize unbelievers. He has been trying, throughout his epistle, to help believers grasp the permanence of their faith (1 Peter 1:3-5) as preparation for the inevitable trials that come with living faithfully in a faithless world (1:6-9,13-25). Peter's audience is already saved. In the immediate context (3:13-17), he reminds them to stay faithful in the event that their good works (3:12,16) generate an injurious response (3:13). Remaining committed to Christ in word and deed during ridicule and persecution (3:14-15) keeps one's conscience free of guilt, a guilt created by compromising a commitment to Christ for the protection of the body (something Peter understood well—Matthew 26:69-75; John 21:15-17).

Just as Noah's faith served him through 120 years of ridicule, so your faith, as expressed or portrayed in baptism, will support you through whatever ridicule you must endure for the sake of the gospel. The image of baptism reminds Peter's audience of their commitment to their imperishable faith, a commitment that will save them from a bad conscience. John Adams (1765), who certainly did not have this passage in mind, nonetheless captured its essence: "Recollect the civil and religious principles and hopes and expectations which constantly supported and carried them [early colonial settlers] through all hardships with patience and resignation." Identification with Christ's death, burial, and resurrection catapults believers through unsought hardships, which just causes naturally provoke (2 Timothy 3:12). Baptism does not save the soul, but memory of it does save or protect the conscience, which is only kept sound or free of guilt by godly living. A good conscience is sustained through a faithful and unrelenting commitment to God.

GPS

1 PETER 4:6

*For the gospel has for this purpose been
preached even to those who are dead,
that though they are judged in the
flesh as men, they may live in the spirit
according to the will of God.*

When and how was the gospel preached to the dead?

The book of Hebrews states "it is appointed for men to die once and after this comes judgment" (Hebrews 9:27). Yet some readers understand 1 Peter 4:6 to mean that the gospel was preached a second time to people who were dead. Proponents of this view tie this verse to a specific understanding of 1 Peter 3:19 and think that this proclamation happened between Jesus' death and resurrection and that He did the preaching. (See the discussion of 1 Peter 3:19.) However, 1 Peter 3:19 and 4:6 are not referring to the same proclamation.

Belief in a second chance for salvation may be emotionally appealing, but it is contrary to everything the Bible teaches about salvation and eternal life. Nowhere does the Bible hold out any hope for salvation and conversion after death.

The emphasis of 1 Peter 4:5-6 is that a day of judgment is coming upon all people whether they are dead or alive. Death does not exempt one from this judgment or invalidate the promises of the gospel. Most people in the ancient world did not believe in accountability after death for all people, and pagan religions did not teach it, but the Bible does.

Every person, Christian and non-Christian, will give an accounting of himself or herself before God. But the Christian's judgment will be different because of faith in Christ. It will not be a judgment because of unbelief.

Peter is not saying the gospel was preached to people after they were dead. Rather, he is declaring that even those who heard and accepted the gospel while they were living but are now dead will receive the benefits of it in eternity. There are present and future benefits of salvation regardless of present circumstances, including persecution and death.

First Peter was written to Christians who were scattered throughout the provinces of Asia Minor (present day Greece and Turkey) and who were undergoing local and personal persecution and suffering because of their conversion from paganism to Christianity. Peter wrote his letter as an encouragement to them, urging them to stand firm in their faith and to live above reproach. He reminds his readers that the message of God's forgiveness and judgment is true for all people in all societies throughout history.

The first-century world was multicultural and pluralistic and shared many attitudes with our world today. The exclusiveness of the gospel and the teachings of Christianity offended many, but Peter encouraged Christians to uphold biblical truth regardless of the cost—even death, for "after you have suffered for a little while, the God of all grace, who called you to His eternal glory in Christ, will Himself perfect, confirm, strengthen, and establish you" (1 Peter 5:10).

TJD

95

A LOT OF SATISFACTION

~ ❋ ~

1 JOHN 2:2

And He Himself is the propitiation for
our sins; and not for ours only, but
also for those of the whole world.

> **How can Christ be the sacrifice for the sins of the**
> **whole world if the whole world will not be saved?**

Before answering the question directly, we need to explain the Greek word *hilasmos* ("propitiation"). Though some have recently promoted the translation "to expiate" (to cover or cleanse from sin), Hellenistic and biblical evidence overwhelmingly suggests that *hilasmos* refers to more than the covering of sin. *Hilasmos* suggests that a sacrifice is being made on the part of a penitent person for the purpose of appeasing or satisfying the gods—defusing their wrath. In the Old Testament, priests offered sacrifices not only to atone for sins, but also to appease God's anger in hope of gaining His favor (Genesis 8:20-22; 2 Samuel 24:17-25; Zechariah 7:2; 8:22; Malachi 1:9). This is propitiation or appeasement. The word is used more than 80 times for this purpose.

The idea that God is angry at sin is disconcerting to some people and has led some to prefer the translation "expiating or cleansing sin." The reasoning suggests that God is not angry at sin, so appeasing Him is unnecessary. The biblical evidence, however, does not support this culturally driven view of God or the translation to which it leads. God's anger at or hatred of sin and its practitioner is so redundant in Scripture that it is hard to imagine how one could miss it (Psalm 5:4-6; Proverbs

6:16-19; Romans 1:18; 2:5,8; 4:15; 9:22; 12:19; 13:4-5; Ephesians 2:3; 5:6; Colossians 3:6; 1 Thessalonians 1:10). God hates sin with a vengeance and sent His Son to "appease, pacify, placate" His anger so that anyone could, through Christ, earn His favor (Romans 5:9-10). His holiness invokes wrath and demands judgment; His amazing love places that judgment on His Son for the benefit of all.

So why isn't everyone saved? The Scripture is clear that Jesus "tasted death for everyone" (Hebrews 2:9) and was sent to be the Savior of the world (1 John 4:14; Acts 4:12). His appeasement of God's wrath is broad enough to include the souls of all humanity, past, present, and future, and is available to both saved and unsaved alike. Believers have His appeasement through Christ as their Savior and Advocate for the purpose of maintaining fellowship with the Lord (1 John 2:1; Romans 8:34); unbelievers have God's appeasement at their disposal for the saving of their souls. It is theirs for the taking. "'Whoever believes in Him will not be disappointed.' For there is no distinction between Jew and Greek; for the same Lord is the Lord of all, abounding in riches for all who call on Him; for 'Whoever will call on the name of the Lord will be saved'" (Romans 10:11-13). The opportunity is universal, but partakers are few (Matthew 7:13-14; 16:15; 1 Peter 3:20; Revelation 22:17).

The reality is that sinful people have the freedom to make up their own minds about God and His plan of salvation. Some people create gods of their own liking, some can't accept their sinfulness, some, for many reasons, haven't heard. But no one will have faith imposed upon him or her. In Christ, all people on the planet have everything they need for eternal salvation, if they will access it through faith and reconciliation. If a person agrees with God about his or her sin and accepts God's solution in Christ, God's wrath is appeased, and he or she acquires the righteousness of God (2 Corinthians 5:18-21). Nobody need be left out—the work is done. Belief is all that remains!

GPS

DEADLY SINS

~ ❀ ~

1 JOHN 5:16

*If anyone sees his brother committing a sin not
leading to death, he shall ask and God will
for him give life to those who commit sin not
leading to death. There is a sin leading to death;
I do not say that he should make request for this.*

> ### Can a Christian commit sins that
> ### are punishable by death?

The answer to this question depends on the kind of death to which John is referring. Is he referring to spiritual death (separation of the soul from God) or physical death (separation of the soul from the body)? Those who understand John to be referring to spiritual death look to his usage of the word in 1 John 3:14 ("passed out of *death* into life," see also John 5:24), where it clearly refers to spiritual death. But interpreters must not be too quick to exclude physical death from the phrase. Salvation in Christ leads us from all manner of death to life: The soul is restored to fellowship with God (spiritual restoration), and the body is guaranteed victory over death and an imperishable state at the resurrection (physical restoration—see 1 Corinthians 15:20-26,53-58). Believers are indeed new creatures in Christ (2 Corinthians 5:14-19).

In the immediate context, John makes this captivating statement: "All unrighteousness is sin, and there is a sin not leading to death (5:17)." We know that the wages of sin is death, both spiritually and physically, with no exceptions (Romans 3:23). Since John cannot be contradicting

Paul, to what death is he referring? Note that John is talking about Christians—those who have already "passed from death to life." He is not talking about the condemnation that comes to all who have sinned, but to a punishment that comes to believers who have committed sins that God considers capital offenses. The sin (or sins—the "a" in the clause "There is a sin leading to death" is not required grammatically) that leads to death does not separate the soul of the believer from God, which would result in the loss of his salvation and nullify the believer's guarantee of physical imperishability. Rather, it results in a divine prerogative that ends the believer's life on earth—a death sentence for which prayer may not provide an acquittal. However, John is not suggesting that we refuse to pray for those who may have committed such sin: "I do not say that he should make request for this." In fact, 1 John 5:16 explains why sins *not* leading to or punishable by death exist—the persistent prayer of fellow Christians. Saints praying for erring or weaker saints save lives (Exodus 32:1-14).

Capital judgments against believers are not unique. Some sins that *can* be punishable by death include: Ananias and Sapphira's deception over the gift of their property to God (Acts 4:32–5:11), behavior that irreparably damages a local church (1 Corinthians 3:16-17), gross immorality (1 Corinthians 5:5; 10:5-10), mishandling of communion (1 Corinthians 10:17–11:34), and, quite possibly, apostasy (embracing doctrines that deny the deity of Christ or that He took on human flesh), which is a major concern of John's (1 John 2:18-24; 4:1-3). What particular sin or sins can provoke a capital response from God is of no concern—hence John's lack of identification—but the knowledge that such an action is possible should stir every believer to pray for those whose faith is weakening through weariness (James 5:15-16) or by the influence of false teaching. John's primary purpose throughout this first epistle is to encourage believers to love each other as God loves them. One natural expression of love should be praying for one another's spiritual growth and overall welfare. Such love may result in the saving of a fellow Christian's life and testimony for the gospel.

GPS

JUDE 9

*But Michael the archangel, when he
disputed with the devil and argued
about the body of Moses, did not dare
pronounce against him a railing judgment,
but said, "The Lord rebuke you!"*

Where does the Bible say that the archangel Michael argued with Satan?

Apart from Satan, the Bible mentions only two angels by name: Gabriel and Michael. According to Daniel 12:1, Michael is a special guardian of the affairs of the nation Israel. And in Revelation 12:7, we are told that Michael and the angels will one day wage war against Satan and his fallen angels, likely at the midpoint of the Tribulation. Only Jude 9 records the unusual confrontation between Michael and Satan over the body of Moses.

Deuteronomy 34:1-6 records Moses' death, but it doesn't mention Satan and Michael struggling over his body. We are simply told that he died on Mount Pisgah, and his burial place is unknown. Many Jewish traditions arose about the death of Moses, but the Bible speaks very little about it. However, there was in Jude's day an apocryphal writing called *The Assumption of Moses* that tells of this conflict. It is not part of the Bible and is now lost except for a small portion. Although not inspired, parts of it may be valid where the contents do not contradict the Bible or biblical doctrine.

Because Jude was writing under the guidance and inspiration of the Holy Spirit, he was not limited to the contents of the Old Testament for historical information. Details that he and other biblical authors included became part of God's inerrant Word once recorded. Biblical authors are not restricted to citing only biblical writings. Even though the extra-biblical writings are not inspired, they may contain true statements. We have no reason to doubt the validity of this conflict between Michael and Satan.

In this verse, Jude argues that if Michael, a mighty archangel, referred a dispute with Satan to the sovereignty of God, thus showing great respect for celestial beings, how much more should mere false teachers show respect for celestial beings. The teachers were wrong in their attitudes and their doctrine.

Jude wrote partly to warn readers about false teachers and innovators who were promoting views and doctrines that were contrary to biblical teaching. He strongly denounces these things and warns against the dangers of mixing true and false teaching. He also warns against becoming indifferent to Bible truths. The false teachers' teachings included a rejection and slandering of the reality and ministry of angels. The Bible does not teach exhaustively about angels, but it does teach of their creation, nature, organization, and ministry. They are very real and important in the Bible and throughout the ages. Nothing in the Bible is insignificant or irrelevant.

Jude's readers uncritically accepted contemporary secular and unbiblical views and mixed them with the teachings of the Bible. John was concerned about this kind of syncretism: "Beloved, do not believe every spirit, but test the spirits to see whether they are from God, because many false prophets have gone out into the world" (1 John 4:1). For first-century Christians, this was a serious problem, and it is in our day as well. Uncritically accepting all teachings and upholding every perspective, opinion, and view as valid compromises God's Word and the significance of the life and ministry of Jesus Christ.

TJD

98

FAIR WARNING

~ ✳ ~

JUDE 14-15

*It was also about these men that Enoch,
in the seventh generation from Adam,
prophesied saying, "Behold, the Lord came
with many thousands of his holy ones to
execute judgment upon all, and to convict all
the ungodly of all their ungodly deeds which
they have done in an ungodly way, and of
all the harsh things which ungodly sinners
have spoken against Him."*

What is this prophecy of Enoch and where is it in the Bible?

Enoch's life and miraculous rapture to heaven without death are found in the Bible (Genesis 5:19-24; Hebrews 11:5-6), but his prophecy is not. His inclusion in the "Hall of Fame" for people of great faith in Hebrews 11 attests to his great spiritual stature. Enoch and Elijah are the only people in the Bible who are taken to heaven without dying. As such, they are precursors of the rapture of the church described in 1 Thessalonians 4:16-17.

Enoch's prophecy is found in a book compiled over a 200-year period just before the birth of Jesus. It is called simply *The Book of Enoch*, and the prophecy of Jude 14-15 is recorded in Enoch 1:9. As in Jude 9, Jude's use of a non-biblical book does not imply that the occurrence is fabricated or that Jude is mistaken. In fact, just the opposite. Because Jude was writing under the inspiration and guidance of the Holy Spirit and was recounting this event as true, we can be certain that it did occur.

Jude is not the only biblical author to cite sources outside the Bible. Paul also did so on several occasions when he quoted from pagan poets (Acts 17:28; 1 Corinthians 15:33; Titus 1:12). In so doing, Jude and Paul are not implying that the books are inspired, only that the truths or events cited are valid.

The judgment of which Enoch prophesied is yet to be fulfilled and relates to the second coming of Christ after the Tribulation (2 Thessalonians 1:7-10). Enoch's prophecy does not give new information to Jude's readers, but at the time Enoch prophesied, this was a very early prophecy in biblical history and is a good summary of the coming universal judgment by God.

Jude is a short book with a strong message. The book exhorts Christians to defend the truth and contend for the faith. It reminds readers that God punishes disobedience and disbelief, citing the Old Testament examples of Cain, Sodom and Gomorrah, the Egyptians, Balaam, and the rebellion of Korah. Jude does not beat around the bush. What you believe and how you live is important to God, and the consequences of your beliefs are eternal as well as temporal.

TJD

IT ALL ADDS UP

~ ✳ ~

REVELATION 13:18

Let him who has understanding
calculate the number of the beast, for
the number is that of a man; and his
number is six hundred and sixty-six.

Why is 666 the mark of the beast, what is it, and what does it mean?

Probably no other number in the Bible or in history has received as much attention and speculation as 666. Revelation 13:16-18; 14:9-10; and 20:4 mention the mark of the beast. During the Tribulation, every person will be required to receive it before conducting any transactions. Every person will receive the same mark, and any person who refuses will be persecuted or killed. This sign of allegiance will affect every part of society.

Giving the mark will be a satanic counterpart to the "sealing" of Christians by God in Revelation 7:2-4, although the word used for *seal* and the word for *mark* are not the same. Like everything the Antichrist does, the mark is an imitation and mockery. Taking the mark will signify commitment and devotion to the Antichrist. The mark will be a visible symbol (on the individual) of the immense power and worldwide authority and control of the Antichrist.

The word for *mark* is similar in meaning to *tattoo* or *brand*. Throughout the Bible, *mark* distinguishes or indicates something by a sign (Leviticus 13:47-59; 14:34-39; Ezekiel 9:4). Religious tattooing was widespread in the Roman Empire and the ancient world, and devotees of a particular god or goddess were often branded or marked to show their devotion. *Mark* was also used for the image or name of the emperor on Roman coins as well as for the seals that were attached to official documents. Similarly, soldiers captured in battle and disobedient slaves often received branding or marking. This was similar to the markings of Jews and others during the Holocaust.

There have been numerous suggestions for the nature of the mark, including an official stamp, an invisible mark (or some technological variation such as a microchip implant), and a branding implant. But the Bible simply doesn't say what it is, except that it is *on* and not *in* people. Likewise, many competing solutions have been offered for identification and understanding of the number, but the Bible does not identify the Antichrist or interpret the number. Instead, it says that when the Antichrist is revealed during the Tribulation, the number of his name—the name's equivalent in numbers—will be 666.

The concept of numerical values associated with names and letters is part of the ancient practice called *gematria*. It is based on the fact that the 22 letters of the Hebrew alphabet were also used as numbers in counting. The first nine letters corresponded to the numbers one through nine, the next nine letters corresponded to tens to ninety, and the last four letters to one hundred to four hundred. Every Hebrew name or word had a numerical significance and the name of the Antichrist, when revealed in the future, will be the numerical equivalent of 666. However, the identification is not yet available, and any speculation as to the identity of the Antichrist before he is revealed is beyond the bounds of legitimate prophetic interpretation.

The Antichrist will use this mark as one of many attempts to mimic the rule of Jesus Christ during the Tribulation. In that regard, it is interesting to note the words of Paul in Galatians 6:17: "From now on let no one cause trouble for me, for I bear on my body the brand-marks of Jesus."

TJD

REVELATION 14:1

I looked, and behold, the Lamb was standing on
Mount Zion, and with Him one hundred and
forty-four thousand, having His name and the
name of His Father written on their foreheads.

Who are the 144,000 people?

The greatest spiritual revival in history is yet to come. According to Revelation 7:1-8 and 14:1-5, 144,000 special witnesses or evangelists will emerge during the Tribulation to proclaim the message of God. These witnesses will have divine protection throughout their ministry to perform service for God in the midst of the Tribulation and reign of the Antichrist.

The 144,000 are not Gentile, but Jewish men, including 12,000 from each of the tribes of Israel. The only tribe missing is Dan, and this omission may be because of the many times that its members were guilty of idolatry (Leviticus 24:11; Judges 18; 1 Kings 12:28-29).

Revelation 14:1 mentions a seal placed on their heads, a counter mark to that of nonbelievers who take the mark of the beast (Revelation 13:16-17). The emblem of recognition for the 144,000 clearly distinguishes them from followers of the Antichrist. They are visually and verbally God's own. The special protection God gives to these witnesses shows the great extent He will go to during this time to bring to faith the maximum number of people (2 Peter 3:9).

Soldiers, servants, and some service people in the ancient world commonly received a visible mark or sign of their devotion to a deity. This conspicuous mark quickly and clearly identified their allegiance and religious devotion to a particular god or goddess. The sign spoken of in Revelation 14:1 will be similar.

Revelation 6–19 provides the greatest amount of information about the Tribulation found in the Bible. The Tribulation will primarily be a time of judgment, but God will extend the gospel of grace and salvation to any who believe. It is a time of punishment for the world's long history of hatred, sin, and rebellion against God (Isaiah 13:9; 24:19-20). But it is also a time of worldwide revival and evangelization (Matthew 24:14). During this time, multitudes of people will turn to God, including many from Israel.

This time of great trauma and tragedy is certain and will follow the rapture of the church. Just as certain, however, is the triumph of those who love Jesus Christ. Present-day Christians should be less concerned about people living in *those* days than people living in *these* days. If you are a Christian, you are to walk in this world in wisdom rather than foolishness, as a wise person rather than an unwise one, "making the most of your time, because the days are evil" (Ephesians 5:16).

TJD

101

A NEW WORLD COMING
~ ❀ ~

REVELATION 21:1

I saw a new heaven and a new earth;
for the first heaven and the
first earth passed away,
and there is no longer any sea.

What is the new heaven and new earth?

John's vision in Revelation provides a detailed and magnificent portrayal of the unfolding of God's prophetic plan. Revelation is filled with specific information about the future of the world and its inhabitants. It was not written to be a source of confusion and controversy, but comfort and consolation. It was written so that Christians might have an incentive to holy living and commitment to Jesus Christ regardless of their circumstances. Revelation reminds us that history is moving toward a time when all of the created order will acknowledge the power and person of God.

Revelation 21–22 contains a description of the eternal state, which commences at the end of the millennium and physical reign of Jesus Christ on earth as described in Revelation 20. In Revelation 21:1, John tells of seeing the new heaven and new earth. This is not a re-creating or remodeling of the present earth and heavens, but a completely new creation. The present creation is like a giant clock set in motion by God that is gradually running down. In God's timing, it will cease and will be replaced by a new and eternal heaven and earth (Matthew 24:35; Mark 13:31; Luke 16:17; 21:33; 2 Peter 3:10-13; Revelation 20:11). The present cosmos is dying and contaminated by sin, but the new heaven and earth that continues throughout eternity will be free of sin.

Surprisingly little information is given about the new heaven and new earth other than the fact that it will have no seas. The new heaven and new earth should not be confused with the millennium, which will have seas and will precede it (Psalm 72:8; Isaiah 11:9,11; Ezekiel 48:28; Zechariah 9:10; 14:8).

One aspect of the new heaven and earth that is mentioned in detail is the presence of the city of New Jerusalem. Revelation 21–22 is very specific and detailed about the city, its inhabitants, and the blessedness of the eternal state. Although many questions about the new earth, the new heaven, and eternity remain unanswered, John's vision leaves no doubt that citizens of the eternal city of New Jerusalem will exist in conditions unlike any known in this world.

Heaven is very real. Today's special effects, fantasy, mysticism, syncretism, and even spiritual apathy can lead people to misrepresent heaven. But the Bible is very clear about its existence and its inhabitants. The new heaven and the new earth are part of heaven and the eternal order. They are also reminders to each of us that for Christians, the best is yet to come. Take care of your soul—you are going to have it for eternity.

TJD

Digging Deeper

Each of the verses summarized in this book is well worth studying more extensively. Listed below are some helpful general reference books about the topics discussed as well as books and articles on specific verses or topics. There is not unanimous agreement among all the works cited below, but each of them does contain a high view of the Bible's inspiration and trustworthiness. Although the list is by no means exhaustive, it is a good starting point, and we encourage you to continue your study of God's Word with these resources.

General Reference Books

Archer, Gleason L., Jr. *Encyclopedia of Bible Difficulties*. Grand Rapids, MI: Zondervan, 1982.

Campbell, Don, et al. *The Theological Wordbook: The 200 Most Important Theological Terms and Their Relevance for Today*. Nashville, TN: Word Publishing, 2000.

Gaebelein, Frank E., ed. *The Expositor's Bible Commentary*, 12 vols. Grand Rapids, MI: Zondervan Publishing, 1978-1991.

Geisler, Norman, and Thomas Howe. *When Critics Ask: A Popular Handbook to Bible Difficulties*. Grand Rapids, MI: Baker Books, 1992.

Grudem, Wayne. *Systematic Theology: An Introduction to Biblical Doctrine*. Grand Rapids, MI: Zondervan, 1994.

Kaiser, Walter C., Jr., et al. *Hard Sayings of the Bible*. Downers Grove, IL: InterVarsity Press, 1996.

Keener, Craig S. *The IVP Bible Background Commentary: New Testament*. Downers Grove, IL: InterVarsity Press, 1993.

LaHaye, Tim, and Ed Hindson, ed. *The Popular Encyclopedia of Bible Prophecy*. Eugene, OR: Harvest House, 2004.

Rhodes, Ron. *What Did Jesus Mean?* Eugene, OR: Harvest House, 1999.

Ryrie, Charles C. *Basic Theology: A Popular Systematic Guide to Understanding Biblical Truth*. Wheaton, IL: Victor Books, 1982.

Walton, John H., Victor H. Matthews, and Mark W. Chavalas. *The IVP Bible Background Commentary: Old Testament*. Downers Grove, IL: InterVarsity Press, 2000.

Walvoord, John F. *Major Bible Prophecies: 37 Crucial Prophecies That Affect You Today*. Grand Rapids, MI: Zondervan, 1991.

Walvoord, John F., and Roy B. Zuck, eds. *The Bible Knowledge Commentary*. 2 vols. Wheaton, IL: Victor Books, 1983, 1985.

Zuck, Roy B. *Basic Bible Interpretation*. Wheaton, IL: Victor Books, 1991.

Specific Studies

Bock, Darrell. *Luke* (2 vol.). In *Baker Exegetical Commentary on the New Testament*, Moisés Silva, ed. Grand Rapids: Baker Books, 1994, 1996.

Boice, James Montgomery. *Psalms: An Expositional Commentary*, 3 vols. Grand Rapids, MI: Baker Books, 1994-1998.

Chisholm, Robert B., Jr. "Does God Change His Mind?" *Bibliotheca Sacra* 152 (Oct.–Dec. 1995): 387-99.

Craigie, P. C. *The Book of Deuteronomy (NICOT)*. Grand Rapids, MI: William B. Eerdmans Publishers, 1976.

Erickson, Millard J. "Is There Opportunity for Salvation After Death?" *Bibliotheca Sacra* 152 (April–June 1995): 131-44.

Grudem, Wayne. "Christ Preaching through Noah: 1 Peter 3:19-20 in Light of Dominant Themes in Jewish Literature." *Trinity Journal* n.s. 7:3-31.

————. "He Did Not Descend into Hell: A Plea for Following Scripture instead of the Apostles' Creed." *Journal of the Evangelical Theological Society* 34:1 (March 1991): 103-13.

Harris, W. Hall, III. "The Ascent and Descent of Christ in Ephesians 4:9-10." *Bibliotheca Sacra* 151 (April–June 1995): 198-214.

Hoehner, Harold W. *Ephesians: An Exegetical Commentary*. Grand Rapids: Baker Books, 2002.

House, H. Wayne. "Apostisia in 2 Thessalonians 2:3: Apostasy or Rapture?" in *When the Trumpet Sounds*, Thomas Ice and Timothy Demy ed. Eugene OR: Harvest House Publishers, 1995: 261-96.

Ice, Thomas, and Timothy J. Demy. *Fast Facts on Bible Prophecy from A to Z*. Eugene, OR: Harvest House Publishers, 1997.

————. *What the Bible Says about Heaven and Eternity* (rev. ed.). Grand Rapids, MI: Kregel Publications, 2000.

Jobes, Karen H. *1 Peter*. In *Baker Exegetical Commentary on the New Testament*, Robert W. Yarbrough and Robert H. Stein, ed. Grand Rapids, MI: Baker Books, 2005.

Lane, William L. *The Gospel of Mark (NICNT)*. Grand Rapids, MI: William B. Eerdmans Publishing Co., 1974.

Merrill, Eugene H. *Deuteronomy*, In *The New American Commentary*, vol. 4., E. Ray Clendenen, ed. Nashville, TN: Broadman & Holman Publishers, 1994.

————. *Haggai, Zechariah, Malachi: An Exegetical Commentary*. Chicago, IL: Moody Press, 1994.

Morris, Henry M. *The Remarkable Record of Job.* Grand Rapids, MI: Baker Books, 1988.

Reaume, John D. "Another Look at 1 Corinthians 15:29, 'Baptized for the Dead.'" *Bibliotheca Sacra* 152 (Oct.–Dec. 1995): 457-75.

Ross, Allen P. *Creation and Blessing: A Guide to the Study and Exposition of Genesis.* Grand Rapids, MI: Baker Books, 1988.

Silva, Moisés. *Philippians* (2nd ed.). In *Baker Exegetical Commentary on the New Testament,* Robert W. Yarbrough and Robert H. Stein, ed. Grand Rapids, MI: Baker Books, 2005.

Thomas, Robert L. *Revelation: An Exegetical Commentary,* 2 vols. Chicago, IL: Moody Press, 1992, 1995.

Waltke, Bruce K. *The Book of Proverbs (NICOT),* 2 vols. Grand Rapids, MI: William B. Eerdmans Publishing Co., 2005.

Walvoord, John F. *The Revelation of Jesus Christ: A Commentary.* Chicago, IL: Moody Press, 1966.

ABOUT THE AUTHORS

Timothy J. Demy has authored and edited more than two dozen books on the Bible, theology, and current issues. He has also contributed to numerous journals, Bible handbooks, study Bibles, and theological encyclopedias. He has been a military chaplain for more than 25 years and served in a variety of assignments with the U.S. Navy, U.S. Marine Corps, and U.S. Coast Guard. He is currently assigned as chaplain at the U.S. Naval War College, where he has also previously taught as an adjunct instructor for many years. He has published and spoken widely on religiously motivated terrorism and the role of religion in international relations.

In addition to his theological training, which he received at Dallas Theological Seminary (Th.M., Th.D.), he holds M.A. and Ph.D. degrees from Salve Regina University, where he wrote about C.S. Lewis. He also earned graduate degrees in European history and national security and strategic studies. He was the President's Honor Graduate from the U.S. Naval War College and is presently a candidate for the degree Master of Studies in international relations at the University of Cambridge.

He is a member of numerous professional organizations, including the Evangelical Theological Society, the Center for Bioethics and Human Dignity, the Society of Biblical Literature, and the Pre-Trib Study Group. He has been listed in *Who's Who in America* and similar volumes and has received numerous awards for his work. He and his wife, Lyn, have been married 28 years.

Gary P. Stewart serves as an adjunct professor at Capital Bible Seminary and Liberty University and has authored and edited 14 books on biblical perspectives in bioethics and other cultural concerns. He has contributed to numerous theological dictionaries, books on biblical studies, journals, and magazines. He has served as a military chaplain for 18 years, serving ashore and afloat with the U.S. Navy, U.S. Coast Guard, and U.S. Marine Corps. He is currently assigned to the U.S. Marine Corps Chemical Biological Incident Response Force.

Gary earned graduate degrees from Trinity Graduate School (M.A. in Bioethics), Grace Theological Seminary (M.Div.), Bethel Theological Seminary (Th.M.), and Western Theological Seminary (D.Min.). He did additional studies at the University of Wales and is currently a Ph.D. student at Liberty University. He has studied broadly in the fields of theology, bioethics, and cultural issues and has been a frequent guest on national television and radio. He is a member of the Evangelical Theological Society, the Center for Bioethics and Human Dignity, and the Pre-Trib Study Group. He is listed in *Who's Who in America* and has lectured widely on current issues. His hobbies include woodworking and music. Gary and his wife, Kathie, have been married 30 years. They have two daughters, Lindsay Anne, who is married to Jeff, and Katie Anne. They have two granddaughters, Lauralyn and Rebekah Kathleen.

Other Great Harvest House Reading

Knowing the Bible 101
Bruce Bickel and Stan Jantz

With extensive biblical knowledge and a contemporary perspective, Bruce Bickel and Stan Jantz provide a manageable approach to understanding God's written message—its origin, themes, truth, and personal relevance.

How to Study the Bible for Yourself
Tim LaHaye

Nationally recognized Bible teacher and author Tim LaHaye releases a 30th anniversary edition of this bestselling guide to help you uncover the wisdom and truth of Scripture for yourself.

Bare Bones Bible Handbook
Jim George

This is the perfect resource for a fast and friendly overview of every book of the Bible. Explores the key themes, characters, events, and verses of Scripture, and highlights important lessons for everyday life.

Christianity According to the Bible
Ron Rhodes

Popular Bible scholar Ron Rhodes lays out the clear teaching of Scripture on 12 essential elements of biblical Christianity. Each chapter is thorough yet easy-to-understand, informative yet highly inspirational.

The Stones Cry Out
Randall Price

Recently uncovered ancient artifacts shed light upon the lives of the patriarchs, the Ark of the Covenant, the fall of Jericho, King David, and more. More than 80 photos demonstrate the incontrovertible facts that support biblical truth.